UNDOCUMENTS

Latinx Pop Culture

SERIES EDITORS

Frederick Luis Aldama and Arturo J. Aldama

UN
DOCU
MENTS

JOHN-MICHAEL RIVERA

THE UNIVERSITY OF
ARIZONA PRESS

TUCSON

The University of Arizona Press
www.uapress.arizona.edu

ISBN-13: 978-0-8165-4003-7 (paperback)

Cover design by Leigh McDonald
Cover photo by JR Korpa
Designed and typeset by Leigh McDonald in Landa 11.5/15.5 and Payson WF [display]

Publication of this book is made possible in part by support from the Calderwood Publication Award.

Library of Congress Cataloging-in-Publication Data
Names: Rivera, John-Michael, 1969– author.
Title: Undocuments / John-Michael Rivera.
Other titles: Latinx pop culture.
Description: Tucson : The University of Arizona Press, 2021. | Series: Latinx pop culture | Includes
    bibliographical references.
Identifiers: LCCN 2020045507 | ISBN 9780816540037 (paperback)
Subjects: LCSH: Mexican Americans—Ethnic identity. | Mexican Americans—Social conditions. |
    United States—Emigration and immigration—Social aspects.
Classification: LCC E184.M5 R583 2021 | DDC 305.8968/72073—dc23
LC record available at https://lccn.loc.gov/2020045507

Printed in the United States of America
♾ This paper meets the requirements of ANSI/NISO Z39.48-1992 (Permanence of Paper).

CONTENTS

TO ACKNOWLEDGE IN THE AGE OF CORONAVIRUS

A specter is haunting the hemisphere, the specter of COVID-19. All the powers of the old regimes have entered into a holy alliance to exorcise this specter: Popes and Presidents, Scientists and Solipsists, Dictators and Progressives, Populists and Racists.

-MARCH 27, 2020-

In quarantine, I listen to Governor Polis of Colorado give a press conference where he ominously describes coronavirus as "a ghost we are all chasing." The end of history seems to have arrived differently than Karl Marx anticipated; the invisible hand of disease erases time with contagion. Confined in our homes during this stay-at-home order, we are all now specters of a specter that haunts us all in our confines as we stare at pixelated outside worlds that document every diseased body, every minute, every hour. I am transfixed by the news ticker running under Wolf Blitzer's mouth: *in new york a person dies every 17 minutes ... 723,000 documented cases confirmed this morning and 20 million projected by next year ... 1 in 3 have covid-19 but don't know it ... dow jones industrial down 13 percent ... a depression is around the corner, says major hedge fund manager.* Like most of you in the spring of 2020, I live and acknowledge in solitude, in fear, in anxiety. I wait for the specter to engulf Colorado. I wait impatiently. So now in the midst of this COVID-19 pandemic, I feel the borders closing around us, made manifest through government actions to shut us off in our homes as well as close both our southern and northern borders. I acknowledge that this pandemic will be used to create yet another document that authorizes the militarization of our borders and the racialization of Others. I acknowledge that the undocumented are dealing with this issue in a much more terrifying manner than I am. They are told by the CDC that they will not be "recorded" if they get tested, but no one trusts a government that uses information like a weapon to incarcerate immigrants. Everyone still remembers Operation Wetback. Everyone still remembers that DACA data was used to deport families. I begin, then, by acknowledging that so many are forgotten and erased in this pandemic that now frames the last words of this book. I acknowledge all of you who are scared, disenfranchised, and forgotten in this strange and terrifying period of our documented history, wherein disease will forever underwrite our lived experiences.

It is against this backdrop that I thank those who have made this book possible. To all who have touched this book in one way or another:

To Norma Cantú, elena minor, Carmen Giménez Smith, Dinty Moore, Robin Hemley, and Harrison Candelaria Fletcher, who were all instrumental in the creation of this project in the very early stages. To Kristen Buckles at the University of Arizona Press, along with Matt Gleeson, whose hand helped every word find its shape, Amanda Krause, Leigh McDonald, and the others who worked on this book and have been supportive at every stage. To the unknown readers of the manuscript who were so insightful and helpful in crafting the edits. To Mark Nowak, who helped me work out early parts of the introduction. To Richard Rodriguez, whose conversations led me to rethink the relationship between craft, identity, and politics. To Cristina Rivera Garza, who inspired me to think through the relationship between writing and death. To Roberto Tejada, who encouraged and read the preliminary poems and helped me realize the manuscript's potential. To my colleagues and friends at WRITE (Writing, Rhetoric,

Information, Technology, and Ecology) Lab, who have been supportive of me as both a writer and the director of the Program for Writing and Rhetoric: John Ackerman, Laurie Gries, Steve Lamos, Eileen Lagman, and our new colleague, Gabi Ríos. To my friend and colleague Jeffrey DeShell, who years ago directed me to experimental books that would inspire me to write this work. To Jimmy Miranda, my graduate student and now colleague, who helped me research parts of this work and inspired with his enthusiasm for thought and ideas. To Andy Fitch, who read an early draft of the work and helped me think about audience. To my friend and colleague Linda Nicita, who was instrumental in making this book possible. With a careful eye she read every page and helped edit this work to its completion. To Julie Carr, my dear friend and collaborator in all things writerly who read every page of many versions, helped guide me through, and encouraged every word, every mark. To my friend Troy Kilen, who sat by me many a time at coffee shops or listened to rambling texts while I tried to work out ideas. His keen wit has been invaluable. To my compadre Phil Joseph, who helped me think through ideas for years and whose friendship has been so important to me over these fifteen years. To Frederick Aldama and Arturo Aldama, who believed in this project from its very early stages and saw, better than I, what it was I was trying to accomplish in this strange hybrid of a book. To my uncle Nick Kanellos, who taught me how to write and later how to navigate academia as a Latinx person. To Emma Pérez, *mi tía*, whose career I emulate in vain, and who introduced me to Gloria Anzaldúa and has been supportive of my writing, always. To my mother, Yolanda, who encouraged every written and read page over the years. This is in some ways a story of our life in documents, and those simulations began with her, in a car heading to Los Angeles with Emma, where she would raise a son on her own, a son who wanted for nothing. I escaped with words and she encouraged each one of them. To my daughter, whom I am so proud of and so happy to get to watch grow up and become such an astute and amazing person, writer, thinker, and athlete. You truly are the best of us all. To my wife, whom I have loved and documented more time with than any person on earth. She has pushed me, encouraged me, and loved me, even during the dark times. I am forever thankful to live my life with you. I love you dearly. And lastly, to my friend in graduate school and then my colleague in Boulder, Vincent Woodard, who died in the first days in which I began this book. Every page is haunted by Vincent, and, like Hamlet's desire to resurrect the words of his ghost, I try to "mark thee," I try to "remember thee" with every word. He was the first to encourage me and tell me that I should take this project on, take chances with my writing, and challenge institutions, genres, and thought with every inscription. I have failed most of the time, but there are moments in this book where I hope I have resurrected his call to mark those unnamed people in the name of justice. "Why else write, why else live?" he would say as we played pool for hours at a local bar, all the time knowing his moments were numbered. I miss him every day, and I hope he knows that I tried. You are missed, Vincent.

PROEM

I watch the play unfold beneath my hands...

GHOST: Mark me!
HAMLET: I will.

. . . .

GHOST: Remember me!
HAMLET: ... Remember thee? / Yea, from the table of my memory / **I'LL WIPE AWAY** all trivial, fond records, / All saws of books, all forms, all pressures past ... Within the book and volume of **MY BRAIN**, / Unmixed with baser matter.

-SHAKESPEARE, *HAMLET*-

PACHUCO: His [pachuco] language, a new creation. ... His will to be an awesome force **ELUDING ALL DOCUMENTATION** *... a mythical, quizzical frightening being ... a precursor of revolution. The pachuco was existential.*

-LUIS VALDEZ, *ZOOT SUIT*-

GENUS DIFFERENTIA

DOCUMENT

>*a piece of written, printed, or electronic matter that provides
>information or evidence or that serves as the official record.*

InDocumentos
(een-doh-koo-mehn-tohs)
[Un]documents / noun:

>*Multi-vocal passage-ware lacking authorized verifications
>regarding entry and/or social identity.*

>*Texts utilized by non-state-actors for mobile existence in-between
>officialized national entities.*

>*A system of undocumented signification of & for the people.*

>*The spoken subject within the context of exile, illegal ID status and/
>or "alien" assignations.*

>*Transgressive acts of perception and interpretation within a
>shifting borderlands territory.*

>*Flux moments in-between being and non-being [Life and Death].*

-JUAN FELIPE HERRERA-

UNDOCUMENTS

PRELUDE

AN INQUIRY

How do you document the undocumented?

undocumented ... undocument the documented ... document the
undocumented ... undocument the documented ... document the
undocumented ... undocument the documented ... document the
undocumented ... undocument the documented ... document the
undocumented ... undocument the documented ... document the
undocumented ... undocument the documented ... document the
undocumented ... undocument the documented ... document the
undocumented ... undocument the documented ... document the
undocumented ... undocument the documented ... document the
undocumented ... undocument the documented ... document the
undocumented ... undocument the documented ... document the
undocumented ... undocument the documented ... document the
undocumented ... undocument the documented ... document the
undocumented ... undocument the documented ... document the
undocumented ... undocument the documented ... document the
undocumented ... undocument the documented ... document the
undocumented ... undocument the documented ... document the
undocumented ... undocument the documented ... document the
undocumented ... undocument the documented ... document the
undocumented ... undocument the documented ... document the
undocumented ... undocument the documented ... document the
undocumented ... undocument the documented ... document the
undocumented ... undocument the documented ... document the
undocumented ... undocument the documented ... document the

undocumented . . . undocument the documented . . . document the
undocumented . . . undocument the documented . . . document the
undocumented . . . undocument the documented . . . document the
undocumented . . . undocument the documented . . . document the
undocumented . . . undocument the documented . . . document the
undocumented . . . undocument the documented . . . document the
undocumented . . . undocument the documented . . . document the
undocumented . . . undocument the documented . . . document the
undocumented . . . undocument the documented . . . document the
undocumented . . . undocument the documented . . . document the

. . . an encyclopedia ought to make good the failure to execute . . .
this inquiry.

–DENIS DIDEROT, *ENCYCLOPÉDIE*–

Fifty-two keys form the alphabet beneath my fingers, sequential punches illuminate the words hidden within the frame. An unnatural union of brain and inanimate touch marks this delicate relationship between my hand and the lettered gray keys. Perfectly squared black pixels frame the outline of knowledge; information flows from mind to plastic to sand to flesh to paper to another body to another eye that gazes upon the page in a world made anew with every entry. The touch of knowledge feels cold, feels dead. A ghost in the machine speaks: "How do you document the undocumented?" This inquiry . . . manically repeated over and over . . . belies the affectual relations that inscribe a ghostly demarcation: undocumented, a word that simultaneously documents, inscribes, and erases; it creates a condition somewhere between the living and the dead, a spectral speech act that reveals the anxious feeling of *being* Latinx since the sixteenth century. To document the undocumented, to undocument the documented, haunts Latinx existence; the inquiry bespeaks a spectral Latinx subject rendered by the shadow of the state, cast and collected by a parchment doppelganger that leaves us split between paper and flesh. This action, this "in-between being and non-being," this is the state of the subject—a mechanism of the state—the logic of our modern information culture, of our, my, anxious age of documentality.

There is an irony buried here within this period of hypervisibility; now, when everything is being catalogued and systematized and more documents are being created than in any other period in history, we are left with an anxious feeling of being perpetually revenant: documented subjects of the nation-state feel and are rendered like ghosts, an absent presence within their own home, a living dead subject haunting a nation-state where documents turn paper to flesh, flesh to paper. And yet, to ask this question—How do you document the undocumented... undocument the documented...?—is both emancipating and repressive; it leaves the subject searching for a mooring that will tether their bodies to a state whose documents write and erase them, a phantasmal logic of necropolitics; we are all re-created in and out of existence, moment to moment, year to year, decade to decade, century to century with a stroke of a pen, the touch of a keyboard.

I document while internalizing paralyzing thoughts of my inevitable death. This feeling, this condition, within this phantasmal body ... my body ... it invokes an anxious feeling of writing under the weight of erasure, what Martin Heidegger described as *écriture sous rature*, and this state of being informs the necessity of creating *UNDOCUMENTS*, modeled, in parts, as a thematic encyclopedia. From Pliny's seminal encyclopedic model to Diderot's affective catalogue of the entirety of Enlightenment thought to Sahagún's colonial New World tome to Hegel's systemization of absolute idealism to Wikipedia's "democratic" all-encompassing Internet project to document the past and future knowledges of the world, encyclopedias rise out of an anxious imperative to document in the face of our future finitude. As d'Alembert relates in his *Preliminary Discourse* to Diderot's encyclopedia, an encyclopedia is an act of humanistic "self-preservation" in the wake of the inevitable "decomposition of bodies." An encyclopedia, then, desires to contain the sands of entropy, "to snatch death from oblivion," as d'Alembert continues to argue, and inscribe a world slipping away from us, to fight human finitude. Encyclopedias are like the last gasp of air we take on our deathbed, moments before the certificate of death is inscribed and catalogued, a life remembered and forgotten with a stroke of a pen and catalogued on a shelf alphabetically.

The *Florentine Codex*, which is the main inspiration and model for *UNDOCUMENTS*, is a haunted text, the first book to organize and document ancient Mexican culture. This book, Sahagún's tomb, was composed in the wake of Spanish colonialism and mass death, and it devoted countless entries to describing death and its rituals. It is important to remember that Sahagún and his Nahuatl compilers wrote frantically while hundreds of thousands of Mexicas were dying from the ravages of colonialism. The work fought not only the erasure of Aztec and Nahuatl knowledge but also the death and extermination of an entire culture. Born out of mass death, the *Florentine Codex* is the first work to reflect the necropoetics of documentality that continues to affect Latinx culture. The first document to catalogue my ancestors haunts my project—it serves as a reminder that colonialism and the Enlightenment organized peoples not only to "preserve" and "archive" their existence but also to bind them within and as documents, as paper ghosts of an ancient long-ago past.

In its cataloguing of Mexica documents, the *Florentine Codex* was the first multivocal encyclopedia to blend genres, themes, styles, and voices, melding and sampling together the poetic language of the Nahuatl flower speakers (*xochitlahtoanime*) with hundreds of images, the codices that were written before, and scholarly scholia of the Enlightenment. Though Diderot would spend pages exploring the relationship between poetics and informatics in his preliminary inquiry, the *Florentine Codex* stands alone in its unique style of imagery, poetics, and documentality. Following the forms and styles of the *Florentine Codex*, UNDOCUMENTS is divided into twelve thematic books (*Gods, Ceremonies, Origins, Soothsayers, Omens, Rhetoric and* **Moral Philosophy,** *The Sun, Moon, and Stars, and the* **Binding** *of* **the Years,** *Kings and Lords, Merchants, The People, Earthly* **Things,** *Con***quest**), each one resurrecting documents that constitute the complicated and contradictory specters of being Latinx.

It should be noted that I am not the first to look to the *Codex* for inspiration. Georges Bataille spent weeks with the *Florentine Codex* while he studied in the seminary, and he used the *Codex's* representation of Aztec ritual, anxiety, and death to inspire his theories of base materialism. The codex, I found, would serve as the model for his own experimental work, *Documents*—an encyclopedia-like work that also remixed poetics, images, and criticism, which he began the same year that he studied the *Florentine Codex*. The *Florentine Codex*, it seems, haunts all of its readers. In the years that followed his fall from the church, Bataille would quote and work from the *Codex* throughout his writings, contemplating "terrifying phantasms" in "Extinct America":

> *The life of civilized peoples in pre-Columbian America is a source of wonder to us, not only in its discovery and instantaneous disappearance, but also because of its bloody eccentricity, surely the most extreme ever conceived by an aberrant mind. Continuous crime committed in broad daylight for the mere satisfaction of deified nightmares, terrifying phantasms, priests' cannibalistic meals, ceremonial corpses, and streams of blood ...*

I resurrect this anecdote because Bataille's *Documents* lurks in the pages of this work, serving as the inspiration for my title, *UNDOCUMENTS*, but his metaphysical relationship to this work should be seen more as spectral. His "base material" use of Aztec culture and sacrifice was ironic at best and racist at worst.

I search for ghosts in the pages of the *Florentine Codex* and the documents that followed, and return to the archives over and over, enacting an inverse version of *redaction theologia*, one that is not searching for the voice of the historical Jesus but rather recovers the subaltern dead voices erased within the parchment. Erasure, then, is recovery. For it is in the erasures that you find the voices of the dead in official documents, buried deep in the parchment and ink. In this way, I follow the groundbreaking work of Mexican artist Teresa Margolles, whose work uses documents to mediate the relationship between the living and dead, asking us "to see what is in the shadows" and inquiring, "There must be some answers in the shadows. When did it start and we didn't notice?" Embracing shadows in *UNDOCUMENTS* is an affectual act of necropoetics, and this recovery leads me to this inquiry: How do you document the undocumented? This, in turn, gives way to the creation of a dying printed form, a dead document in the age of pixelated wonder, the encyclopedia, a wailing disembodied collection of metonymic entries that partially resurrect the traces that lie buried beneath the archives of the state, undocumented specters that emerge when the eyes' mind focuses on the refractions of the obliterated that surround us all daily.

UNDOCUMENTS catalogues, remixes, recovers, and erases documents and images by and about peoples of Greater Mexico, from ones dating back to roughly the first colonial moments when ancient New World Mexican peoples were organized and documented—in the *Florentine Codex* (1592)—to those from our current Wiki Age, wherein President Trump imposes his desires to classify, deport, and erase Latinx immigrants from this anxiety-ridden and engulfing documentary culture. The thematic focus is the necropoetics of Greater Mexican documentality itself—that is, the book is concerned with the complicated and contradictory ways in which peoples of Greater Mexico have been documented and undocumented within necropolitical systems of colonial knowledge and rendered as specters of the state, an act of what Derrida identifies as hauntology. The irresolvable tension between inscription and erasure frames each entry. This duality does not produce a passive Greater Mexican subject. As the documents I present in this work show, the undocumented subject haunts the ideological state apparatus, which feeds on documents that are needed to exercise control over mortality and life, and calls attention to the spectral logic of undocumentality because it reveals its need for bodies, both living and dead, rendered through and as paper.

UNDOCUMENTS looks at the necropoetics of Greater Mexican undocumentality, then, with an eye toward what Chicana theorist and poet Gloria Anzaldúa imagined as la facultad, which is a poetic and affective capacity to see in surface phenomena the meaning of deeper realities, to see the deep structure below the surface. La facultad enables the materialization of the spectral within documents that at face value give life through state authority and decree. La facultad opens my pineal eye, my third eye; it enables me to see the phantasmagorical that is not rendered at first glance. Finding reason within the spectral logic of the document is made possible through Anzaldúa's facultad and, similarly, what Bataille argued for in Dossier of the Pineal Eye (Dossier de l'oeil pinéal), which I read as a metaphysical way of "seeing the dead." Bataille argued that such vision was possible through a secretion of the pineal body, a way of seeing the spectral, absent presences within the material, within the ink of the Enlightenment. Let us not forget that, for Anzaldúa, Bataille, and Derrida, the specter is both material and immaterial, living and dead, resurrected through the register of decay. What Anzaldúa's facultad and Bataille's pineal eye enable me to see are Nietzsche's "phantasms linked with phantasms," documents with documents. I am haunted by visions of linked dead documents.

In this rendering of linked dead documents, I must confess now that *UNDOCUMENTS* is by no means complete or comprehensive; this work is as partial and fleeting as the spectral subject that it tries to represent. The entries in its books are metonymic and reveal historical snapshots of various lengths, and different images, ghosts, and erasures, primarily focused on the peoples and spaces of Greater Mexico; people who have been erased from institutional knowledge; people who have been born, murdered, reborn, and murdered again with a stroke of a pen and then catalogued as a document. *UNDOCUMENTS* resurrects the erased and erases the inscribed, formed as what Anzaldúa has modeled as an assemblage, a montage, *a beaded work with several leitmotifs and with a central core, now appearing, now disappearing in a crazy dance.*

*

I owe the discovery of Uqbar to the conjunction of a mirror and an encyclopedia.... *The mirror hovered, shadowing us.*

–JORGE LUIS BORGES–

How do you document the undocumented? Jorge Luis Borges's work was centrally interested in this question. Indeed, I would go so far as to say that all of his speculative fictions took documentality and information systems as central foci, and, as such, he created an aesthetics of documentality that should be read by all information theorists. One story that has captured my imagination as I think through documentality is "Tlön, Uqbar, Orbis Tertius," which, for me, reveals the encyclopedic visions rendered by aesthetics of undocumentality. Inspiring many an encyclopedic project, from Tisa Bryant's *Encyclopedia* to the Zweite Enzyklopädie von Tlön, this speculative fiction, related as a first-person narrative, focuses on the discovery of an undocumented world envisioned through an encyclopedia that the author recovers through *the conjunction of* a haunted mirror and material documents, a melding of the phantasmatological and the material. This haunting leads to a recovery of the mirrored world of Tlön, whose inhabitants are completely idealistic and live imagined lives that, as the pages progress, shadow the "real" world. The work is one of the first to speculate on the interdependent roles of encyclopedism, documentality, and haunting in world-making. Moreover, Borges's "Tlön" is one of the first texts to critique the modern rise of documentality, the information age, as a "mirroring" totalitarian act. His is a critique of state-sponsored totalitarianism whose citizens are inscribed and erased through documents controlled by authoritarian regimes. The plot centers on how "undocumented countries" like Uqbar are constituted by all-engulfing information systems that hide totalitarian authority through what Borges describes as a "monstrous mirroring," or what Georges Bataille calls the spéculaire in his analysis of mirrors and phantoms, or what Derrida defines as *hauntology*.

In this way, Borges is interested in the authoritative and "hovering" metaphysical effect of documents, the ways in which documents mirror and haunt the world (the first sentence of the story, *I owe the discovery of Uqbar to the conjunction of a mirror and an encyclopedia*, highlights this), and the power of the document in distorting an image of the world and ironically turning subjects into specters, haunted objects of totalitarian organization systems. For Borges, the encyclopedia is that perfect vessel of phantasmal authority; it is a form that creates and circulates, conspicuously from door to door, documents that are able to make worlds emerge and recede through a logic of the *spéculaire*, a constant reproductive reflection of reality that is unable to tether itself to a material worldview. The story further develops as the narrator searches for documents of an "undocumented country" and the secret regimes that created Tlön, which in time becomes a doppelganger, a specter if you will, of the world of the narrator. Tlön haunts, and, like the conjunction of the encyclopedia and the mirror, Tlön and the narrator's world eventually conjoin in a phantasmal struggle with reality. What Borges captures in 1941 is the modern concept of documentality, the spectral effect of documents that simultaneously resurrect and kill a world's knowledge in order to create and maintain power within democratic systems whose lungs rely on information to breathe. His story reveals the ironies of the information age; that is, to live in a recorded world, to live in a world of documentality, is to live in a world of specters, a world of ghosts demarcated through paper.

✳

As with all people made of paper, there was no official record of Merced de Papel's death, no death certificate, or funeral announcement; even the accident report refused to acknowledge her.

–SALVADOR PLASCENCIA, *THE PEOPLE OF PAPER*–

How do you document the undocumented? To answer this, one must acknowledge that to live in a world that desires to catalogue and organize knowledge is also to live in a world that desires to turn migrant bodies into paper ghosts, into the living, wandering dead. Salvador Plascencia's *The People of Paper*, a work under the anxiety of Borges's influence, explores how and why Latinx immigrant peoples have become undocumented specters, without "death certificates or documents that acknowledge," of a documented world controlled by invisible documenters. The character that begins and haunts the work, Merced de Papel, is literally bound together with the "leaves of Leviticus and Judges," and created not from "the rib of man" but from "paper scraps," brought to life from "dead letters." Set up as a metaphor for the relationship that immigrants have to a world of paper, Merced de Papel wanders within the pages of the novel, a migrant paper ghost, the inscribed dead, searching for the pulp that will resurrect her as whole. This immigrant act of inscribing and ultimately erasing the body through paper leaves her endlessly searching, partial and fleeting; she walks off the pages as a dissolved memory, a ghost, whose "history was one on the lips of lovers, the scars that parted their lips."

Merced de Papel's embodied textuality renders the question "How do you document the undocumented?" and illuminates the fact that papers marked by the living and the dead constitute Latinx peoples, but nevertheless the subject is left constantly searching for pulp, trying to escape the surveillance of the state that catalogues them daily in order to regulate and engulf them in a world of surveillance. From Operation Wetback to Operation Gatekeeper, from the RAISE Act to the DREAM Act, from E-Verify to other equally insidious anti-immigration acts of 2019, immigrants of Greater Mexico have been catalogued by the state with their every move. Paper engulfs all Latinx communities, both the documented and the undocumented. In the end, Plascencia's novel imagines a utopian resolution to documentality. Merced de Papel challenges the omnipotent authority of the narrator and leaves the pages that document her body, while still remaining an absent plot-driving presence through her haunting. To escape the authority that renders documents like Merced de Papel is to escape the invisible hand of the state that inks documents into people and people into documents. She is able to attain undocumentality, an emancipated state outside the bureaucratic eye of the panopticon.

*

Paper is paradoxical; it not only inscribes existence, gives life, but also simultaneously renders the body as a trace object of the information age, a dead document. While we live in a world that catalogues every document and creates wiki pages for every moment, we also live in a world where real flesh-and-blood people are made and unmade as inanimate lifeless documents. Documenting is that action—the complicated and contradictory ways in which Latinx peoples are made into living dead subjects who are simultaneously erased through the very paper that points to their existence. This is the colonial power of paper in the information age, of the circulating document—for, buried within its rhetoric, rendered in its representational powers, within the ink, within the very pulp of the document itself, every document has the desire to constitute its object as a living ghost, a specter. Documents, then, resurrect the social imaginary, as Maurizio Ferraris would have us believe, but they do so by rendering the subject partial and fleeting, the living dead, to borrow from Mbembe's work on the necropolitical. They are in an in-between state, fighting to resolve this tension that causes anxiety. The document, then, creates a specter, who, in the pineal eye of Bataille and the playful hand of Derrida, exceeds ontological oppositions between absence and presence, visible and invisible, living and dead. It is no surprise, then, to learn that Greater Mexican people have in the public spheres been labeled the "invisible [ghostly] minority."

With the Treaty of Guadalupe Hidalgo in 1848, Mexicans were constituted as hyphenated subjects; that treaty, according to Juan Gómez-Quiñones, is a foundational document that attempts, but fails, to define the fleeting and partial existence of "Mexican-Americans" in the United States, for its provisions concerning Mexican subjectivity were never ratified. The result of the treaty's failures, as Plascencia later shows us all too well, is that to live as a Greater Mexican person in the information age is to live as a spectral subject, a subject cast into an undocumented purgatory. The person is *sin papeles* but is simultaneously an inscribed object of government authority, an authority wherein thousands of paper documents constitute the racial subjectivity of Greater Mexican subjects as all too material and fleshly for the "democratic" desires of documentality. Plascencia's conjuring of these migrant paper ghosts, and Borges's "mirrors," reveal how the trope of haunting is used by Latinx artists to call attention to the spectral logic of documents and the complicated ways in which Latinx peoples have embraced and resurrected the papered dead in a nation-state where paper inscribes democratic norms. The ghost is not silent, is not passive; it is revenant; it does not return as the object of colonialism but rather haunts colonialism hidden within democracy; it calls attention to its documentality regimes. Haunting ruptures with its wailing, commanding us, like Hamlet's ghost, to "mark me . . . ," "remember me . . . ," and inscribe their justice.

*

A BILL

To amend the Immigration and Nationality Act to establish a skills-based immigration points system, to focus family-sponsored immigration on spouses and minor children, to eliminate the Diversity Visa Program, to set a limit on the number of refugees admitted annually to the United States, and for other purposes. This Act may be cited as the "Reforming American Immigration for a Strong Economy Act" or the "RAISE Act" striking

Striking   striking   strike   Striking

striking strike, Striking   striking striking strike

Striking striking strike   Striking striking strike, Striking

striking striking   striking strike   Striking

striking   strike   Striking striking strike Strike

striking striking striking striking

strike Striking   striking strike   Striking

striking strike   Striking   striking   strike

Striking striking striking striking

striking strike   Striking   striking

striking   striking

is amended by striking.

How do you document the undocumented? Fifty-four times Trump's 2017 RAISE Act legislates this answer through the word *strike*. *Striking* so emphatically in order to erase the laws of the past with a stroke of a pen, the RAISE Act attempts to strike millions of immigrants from our landscape, who now will be barred or deported after finding that they do not qualify for entry. I take the RAISE Act test. I fail.

You don't qualify to apply

Your score: 26 | Minimum score: 30

You must be at least 18 years old and have at least 30 points to be eligible to apply for immigration, according to proposed legislation.

I would not be allowed to enter the United States if I were trying to enter today in 2017. I can't forget that I have the privilege of taking the test as a documented hyphenated subject, a "Mexican-American," and yet many of *mi gente* and extended *familia* do not have this opportunity. They are forced, after the removal of DACA, or after being "stricken" by the RAISE Act and other historical documents, to hide in the shadows of the information age when documents they were told would free them from obscurity, from invisibility, failed to inscribe them. This question, then—"How do you document the undocumented?"— for me, is deeply personal. Is deeply contradictory. Is deeply hypocritical. For me, it emerges out of time, circumstances, geography, fate, and the colonialism and neocolonialism that have made it possible for me to write this book as a documented Mexican of the United States. Born in 1969 to Mexican parents, both of whom spent time in the fields of El Campo, Texas, I was documented by my birth certificate as "Caucasian." A circumstance of documentary racial history. It is important to point out that at that time Mexicans were not "a documented race" in Texas, despite having been murdered and racialized since Texas's annexation in 1836. When I was born, segregation and the racialization of Mexicans, both documented and undocumented, were the harsh reality in Pasadena, a city built upon refineries outside of Houston, Texas. The bracero program, which made it possible for some of my family to come to the United States, had just ended, and Operation Wetback was also in its last iterations. There were swimming pools that I still could not swim in and barbers where I could not get my hair cut, and the residues of Jim Crow were still clinging to more subtle information networks. Today I am awarded a passport, and with it a pamphlet that directs me, "The world is yours." I can travel from state to state and country to country because of my circumstances of documentality. As much as I am a part of a large Latinx community, I am very aware that we are categorized differently because of documents, given inscription or erased because of paper that governments legislate.

Writing forty-seven years after I was certified living, now in this "Documentary Wiki Age," when Trump and his administration saturate the public spheres with propaganda about immigrants in order to subjugate and control knowledge about "Mexican rapists," "murderers," "animals," and those "not human," I begin this prelude and the final edits of this book's entries on the day Trump signs an executive order to deport millions of Latinx immigrants, and when nearly a million DACA recipients are now put into legal jeopardy, a six-month state of limbo while awaiting new legislation. Now Latinxs are relegated to an information-age purgatory before they are located and deported using the very documents that promised to give them presence and security. So, I cannot forget that I begin the pages of this book during yet another period of crisis for immigrant Latinxs in the United States—sadly, one of many that I will try to recover in order to call attention to the complicated ways Latinx peoples have been undocumented in U.S. cultures. Perhaps the irony is that I begin this encyclopedic project to document the undocumented, to recover and make visible the erased

STATE OF TEXAS

TEXAS DEPARTMENT OF HEALTH
BUREAU OF VITAL STATISTICS

TEXAS DEPARTMENT OF HEALTH
REC'D SEP 10 1969
BUREAU OF VITAL STATISTICS

CERTIFICATE OF BIRTH   BIRTH NO. 142-69 100xxx

STATE OF TEXAS

1. PLACE OF BIRTH		2. USUAL RESIDENCE OF MOTHER (Where does mother live?)	
a. COUNTY Harris		a. STATE Texas	b. COUNTY Harris
b. CITY OR TOWN (If outside city limits, give precinct no.) Pasadena		c. CITY OR TOWN (If outside city limits, give precinct no.) Pasadena	
c. NAME OF HOSPITAL OR INSTITUTION (If not in hospital, give street address) Pasadena Memorial Hospital		d. STREET ADDRESS (If rural, give location) 2734 Lilac	
d. IS PLACE OF BIRTH INSIDE CITY LIMITS? YES ☒ NO ☐		e. IS RESIDENCE INSIDE CITY LIMITS? YES ☒ NO ☐	f. IS RESIDENCE ON A FARM? YES ☐ NO ☒

| 3. NAME (Type or Print) | (a) First John | (b) Middle Michael | (c) Last Rivera | 4. DATE OF BIRTH 7-2-69 |
| 5. SEX Male | 6a. THIS BIRTH SINGLE ☒ TWIN ☐ TRIPLET ☐ | 6b. IF TWIN OR TRIPLET, WAS CHILD BORN 1st ☐ 2nd ☐ 3rd ☐ | | 8. COLOR OR RACE White |

7. NAME	(a) First Johnnie	(b) Middle (None)	(c) Last Rivera	8. COLOR OR RACE White
9. AGE (At time of this birth) 22 YEARS	10. BIRTHPLACE (State or foreign country) Texas	11a. USUAL OCCUPATION Airman Basic	11b. KIND OF BUSINESS OR INDUSTRY U.S. Air Force
12. MAIDEN NAME	(a) First Yolanda	(b) Middle (None)	(c) Last Perez	13. COLOR OR RACE White
14. AGE (At time of this birth) 21 YEARS	15. BIRTHPLACE (State or foreign country) Texas	16. CHILDREN PREVIOUSLY BORN TO THIS MOTHER (Do NOT include this child)		
		a. How many OTHER children are now living? 0	b. How many OTHER children were born alive but are now dead? 0	c. How many children were born dead (fetal deaths after 20 weeks pregnancy)? 0

17. INFORMANT Yolanda Rivera		
18. I hereby certify that this child was born alive on the date stated above	19a. ATTENDANT'S SIGNATURE N. L. Powers	19b. ATTENDANT AT BIRTH M.D. ☒ D.O. ☐ MIDWIFE ☐ OTHER ☐
	19c. ATTENDANT'S ADDRESS N. L. Powers, M.D. 4040 Red Bluff Rd. Pasadena, Texas	19d. DATE SIGNED 7-3-69
at 2:25 A ── M		
20a. REGISTRAR'S FILE NO. 1286	20b. DATE REC'D BY LOCAL REGISTRAR 8-12-69	20c. REGISTRAR'S SIGNATURE W.C. Mays

This is to certify that this is a true and correct reproduction of the original record as recorded in this office. Issued under authority of Rule 54a, Article 4477, Revised Civil Statutes of Texas.

ISSUED OCT 2 3 1985

W.D. Carroll
W D CARROLL
STATE REGISTRAR

WARNING: IT IS ILLEGAL TO DUPLICATE THIS COPY.

CERTIFICATION OF VITAL RECORD

documents that define Latinx peoples, in the United States, where everything is being documented, through paper or electronic means, in order to document our people as the living dead.

*

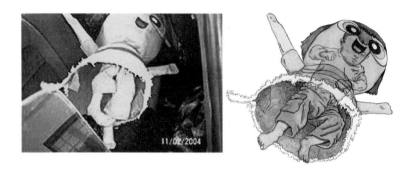

11/02/2004

It is not an agreeable fate to be haunted without respite by one's own image.

-GEORGES BATAILLE ET AL., *ENCYCLOPAEDIA DA COSTA*, 1947–

I am haunted by this blurred image, by this boy created by burning light onto paper. I am haunted by the photograph of this boy, this faceless boy I presumed at first to be dead, whom an ICE (Immigration and Customs Enforcement) agent registered for the official state record, now wandering with the thousands of undocumented dead whose pixelated bodies endlessly roam within haunted big-data systems. Alive or dead, he is now a documented ghost in the machine. The Enlightenment, which gave birth to documents like this, fights this haunting. It tells me to relinquish this anxious feeling to reason. But I am still haunted by a face I cannot see, and anxiety engulfs my being, takes over my body as I write these pages. I see myself in this document, this photograph. I see my death certificate. I see my death, which I have feared my whole life, and which has rendered me frozen in a self-imposed purgatory. I am reminded of Susan Sontag, who told us that there is an inextricable link between photography and one's own death that haunts people; photographs are "memento mori that enable participation in another's mortality." This haunting makes me feel anxious, selfish, guilty, indulgent in my own anxiousness about my mortality as a Mexican man who has lived in the United States forty-five years longer than this boy. I still breathe, even if I experience the constant skipped heartbeats caused by adrenaline racing from the image's punctum to my body. I cannot forget that at his age I traveled from Texas to California, with official documents in hand, a journey that would change my mom's, my aunt's, and my own lives forever. Now in L.A. in 2011 my guilt gives way to anger when I see Julio Morales's *Undocumented Interventions*, curated for the *Phantom Sightings* exhibition at LACMA, which makes me see the power in haunting, giving me this boy's face. His work helps me confront my guilt and search for justice for this young boy; I ask if his ghost can be heard, can be seen by others, can challenge reason through his absent presence. I ask this of myself. I ask this of you. I think, I see, I *inscribe* anxiously *sous rature* . . . under the weight of this erasure . . .

BOOK I
Gods

Reading antiquity of his people   it is likely that more than a thousand
years went by   before it was destroyed   this land was populated
the knowledge or wisdom of this people   was considerable   per-
fect philosophers   were constructed   Our Lord God intended the
depopulated land be settled   I pause to relate riddles   these people
our brother   the stock of Adam   taught in these sciences

YOU A READER

When this work began, it began to be said by those who knew of it, that
a dictionary was being made.
How does this dictionary progress?

It is impossible for me to prepare a dictionary

I have laid groundwork

arranged columns
A clear copy

not finished

language aid me
knowledge

is language

with all of its secrets

BERNARDINO DE SAHAGÚN

This work is like a dragnet to bring to light all the words of this language with their exact and metaphorical meanings, and all the ways of speaking, and most of their ancient practices, the good and evil.

-BERNARDINO DE SAHAGÚN, 1578-

Bernardino de Sahagún was a Franciscan missionary to the Aztec Nahuatl people of Mexico, best known as the compiler of the *Florentine Codex*, also known as *Historia general de las cosas de Nueva España* (*General History of the Things of New Spain*); the actual dates of Bernardino de Sahagún's birth and death are unknown, though some believe he was born in Sahagún in 1499 and died in what is now Mexico City in 1590. This we believe. We do not know what he truly looked like, although, as with the son of his God, Jesus, there are thousands of pictures and hundreds of statues bearing his likeness. We are not even sure if he wrote the first encyclopedia of the New World, the *Florentine Codex*, the first book of knowledge that describes things Greater Mexican, things unknown to him, terra incognita, to us, then . . .

*

Tlatelolco, 1590: Sahagún died in 1590, but this was not the first time. As he lies prostrate with pus-filled lungs, now unable to move, his physicians tell him: Your time has come. Barely breathing, he writes his last commandment: *My hour has not yet arrived*. Like Saint Francis, he will prophetically know the moment when time stops.

A monument and plaque now register his life:

> **León, Spain, 1966—Fray Bernardino de Sahagún / Sahagún 1499–1590 / Missionary and educator of the people / The Father of Anthropology in the New World / Day of the Region of León / 2 June 1966 / The Province of León / To Fray Bernardino de Sahagún, Sahagún XI–VI MCMLXVI**

He calls his disciples, young Nahuatl compilers of the *Florentine Codex*, to his deathbed; they sing songs to conjure the corporeal body into an immortal ghost, a saint of New World knowledge. He looks at them—a failure—for his codex is not quite complete. No longer in his possession, the codex is now an ornamental object for King Philip II, a gift to his nephew on his wedding day. Other scribes used the copies to wrap spices for the lovers of the conquest. Others just burned it. Now ashes. Too much knowledge for its time. The first encyclopedia that would challenge the divinity of God, the idea of the Other, of terra incognita, is lost; the remains today now in Florence a remnant of a relic. In the last moments, a life unfulfilled, a work still incomplete, he still wonders: Was it their codex? Their hand? Was I able to explain away the unknown? Can I inscribe my name on the pages, even now?

He began the composition of the *Florentine Codex* in August 1576, but really it found its first breath when His word could not explain the new world. Never alone, then, he stares at the bloodstained *amatl* drafts, slowly creating three columns, one in Nahuatl, another in Castilian Spanish, and the last of Latin scholia, factual marginalia that help elucidate the sometimes flowery prose and digressions of his hand and the hands of others, which have now decayed within the dirt of terra incognita.

Then a great sickness, *huey cocoliztli*, infected all of them. The fevers were contagious, fiery, and continuous; all were pestilential and, in large measure, lethal. The tongue, black and dry. Intense thirst; the urine sea-green, but now and again turning a pale color. Rapid and frequent pulse, but faint and weak, sometimes even null, only to be resurrected with a gasping breath. The eyes and entire body, yellow. And the delirium and convulsions; boils behind one or both ears; a hard and painful tumor; pains in the heart, chest, and abdomen; shaking and great anguish and dysentery. The blood flowing from cut veins was very pale green, dry and without serosity. The lips gangrenous, the pudenda and other regions of the body now putrefying members; many had hemorrhaging ears and noses; those who fell ill hardly ever recovered. Many were saved by bleeding from the nose. The Aztec compilers etch a picture:

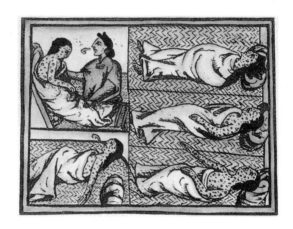

The rest perished. He did not die, though he would be ill most of his remaining days while he finished the codex. One would think this is irony, the birth of "New World" knowledge during the death of a people. For him, it is not. For him, knowledge finds its breath in that last gasp, that quicksonic moment when life gives way to death. Sacred desires led him to his pages, to the pressed and scented *amatl*, to write what was fleeting and partial, an old world made anew through his hand. His experiences in this world, its birth, its death, inscribed through experiences material to his touch, smelled through his nose, seen through his eyes, alone now. Where does this leave his sacred devotion, his calling by God, first heard five thousand miles away in the city of Sahagún? His Father . . . his God . . . left his mind years ago. Can he hear divinity here in the New World, now whispers . . . echoes lost within calderas created within the batholiths hiding behind his eyes? Here in this "New World" he thinks he heard Him, his God, say,

"Guide My hand." He let His hand guide his to document, but never too long. Blasphemy to Him . . . not now. He cannot hear that now. Just whispers of judgment around him. His knowledge of a world that His language could never really grasp allows him to gather the strength to ponder a book, his life's work, his life, the codex. His knowledge, my God. Old, feeble, near death, he realizes his codex is now gone, taken to a world where decoration subsumes their obligation. His last thoughts . . . Whose authority do I resurrect in these documents? Who will read it now?

*

We will always wonder what, in this **mal d'archive**, he may have burned. We will always wonder, sharing with compassion in this archive fever, what may have burned of his secret passions, of his correspondence, or of his "life." Burned without him, without remains and without knowledge. With no possible response, be it spectral or not, short of or beyond a suppression, on the other edge of repression, originary or secondary, without a name, without the least symptom, and without even an ash.

-JACQUES DERRIDA, ARCHIVE FEVER-

I try to make documents from the ashes of a past I never lived. I think I remember it like this but memories, like ash, dissipate with the winds of time. This was my childhood, and that person now is as unknown to me as Sahagún's God.

Lankershim Blvd., CA, 1977: Manuel Martínez de Sahagún died in 1977. (No plaque was created, no tombstone placed.) His name now ash in my memory. I think he died on a Tuesday, but I know this was not the first time. Coal smoke filled his lungs in 1918, sucking the oxygen from his body. Somehow, though the facts were never clear to me, he died for five minutes during a battle on the border between New and Old Mexico. In short bursts of memory, he told me the story the first time, and I think it sounded like this . . .

In 1918 I was on a train, pushing coal into an engine to make steam fast enough so that we could get to Columbus, New Mexico; we were going to fight the U.S. government, but that is a story for another time; weeks before, the coal man Francisco was shot in a bar in Juárez, so they put me up front. I was never that useful. Villa always had me filling in when someone died or did not want the work. I never really was part of the Villistas. My real job, though, was to be Pancho Villa's collector; Villa knew he was an important part of history; when the man from Hollywood—wait, this was before they called it Hollywood, I forgot the place name; but he came down to Mexico to film Villa's Battle of Ojinaga in 1914; his name was Frank Thayer; a pretty decent guy, but no real understanding of Mexico, just its violence; Villa told me to watch Thayer and make sure he captured the real him. I learned a lot—mostly, though, that moving pictures never capture anything more than dust, smoke, and death. Villa hated what he saw—he did not think that was the real him, so Villa kicked Frank out of Mexico; and I was left to burn the film reels; they are still looking for them, you know; Thayer kept what he called the "hard edits," but I kept a whole reel; it's somewhere in this apartment; that was my last job as Villa's archivist, to burn images. Sad but true. I have tried for years to write about this, but the words never seem to flow like time passed; our past time; after the battle was lost, I was left with no real work, no purpose, and somehow Villa associated me with Thayer; Villa did not think he should be captured on page or on film anymore; these were the last days, the hard days when death framed all of our actions; so he put me in the front of the train. I was never a strong man (I was sick as a child and my breathing always hard), so hauling coal was tough for me; Villa knew this. I think he wanted me to leave, but like all of us, he gave me that choice; well, some of us; he did kill a few, you know. I had been with him for years, and we both knew the same familia in Chihuahua when he was governor, so we had history. I wrote for the local paper and wrote about Villa; back then it was all good because his fight really was for the people; when the pobres needed money and the central government would not make jobs or help us out, Villa just printed it, money, made up so many thousands and handed it out like candy; that is another story, though. OK, so this is how I died: while steaming to New Mexico to fight the pinches americanos, me and Francisco's boy, the man who got shot in a bar in Juárez, Miguel, were putting coal in the chute as fast as we could—bullets were flying everywhere—if you are going to stop a train you always fire at the people who are fueling it— and Miguel was shot and when he was shot he flung back his arms and somehow hit my head with his shovel (you should see those shovels as big as a wheelbarrow), and I flew forward and then I burnt my hands—see, here are the scars—and that was when I sucked up a big whiff of coal dust—I passed out and everyone said I died for ten minutes; when I woke up Villa was standing over me laughing; "Ride with me from now on so you don't kill yourself doing a man's work; your grandmother will kill me well before the government does if I let you die," he said; a few things happened after that that don't really matter anymore, and I can't remember now, but maybe I will tell you later when I find the things around here that help me remember; what you need to know is that over the next week I realized that my time had passed in Mexico,

BERNARDINO DE SAHAGÚN   31

and so I went to California. I never returned to Mexico; some long for their birthplace, I never have; still haven't; Villa died a few years later. I was not there to write it down or see it, so I am not so sure if this is true or not. I have heard that he lived for another fifty years back in Chihuahua, living among the people he helped free. My grandmother said he came to her taquería and asked for me. I believe this sometimes; hard to know what really happened back then; life went too fast to capture it all; now let's go look for Thayer's broken reel. I know it's here somewhere.

✳

Sahagún Jr. lived in that apartment for twenty years, the first tenant. A native of Chihuahua, Mexico, Sahagún Jr. moved to California alone—like us. We had recently left Texas—a vacation still unfolding—Disneyland E tickets to enter It's a Small World now create a small apartment complex in North Hollywood, one hundred yards from the 118, where we paid weekly—I called that home for the first years—the time between my father, my mother's men after him, and the others I recalled as . . . Brown stucco, two stories high, we lived on the bottom floor—she managed to manage the place, collecting rent, collecting belongings from those left behind by those who left, those now dead. Sahagún's apartment was laid out like ours—not allowed to enter at first—I picture him lying on the floor. Gray hair matted, skin blue, no signs of pain, just the smell of drying flesh, now the dust outlines where a body once lay. The smell of all his things, of skin, of dander, of dust fills my lungs, sucks the oxygen from my body, dizziness—a fever develops, caused by the history taken in through the nose. Things break down in the air, carrying traces of the fingers that once touched them—held by their own. Did it suffocate him, the touch, my gaze upon his things, his dead body, still haunting me? I still have Derrida's archive fever.

In my mind I had been in his house over fifty times. What I knew then was that he had been a librarian at the Lankershim branch, and after he retired he had managed to create a library of things, an archive of himself and all things known as Mexican. He charged us kids five cents, or we had to write a story, to enter and look around. "You have to pay for knowledge," he would tell us. We could check things out overnight, but none of us ever did. I wrote stories to get in, but most of the time he told me they were not worth five cents. I'll tell you a story, he said, and told me to keep trying. I'll let you in today, but have your mom take five cents off my rent. I never knew what to think; everything was story, everything was still untold, unknown.

Sahagún's apartment: a spatial encyclopedia. He had managed the unthinkable: to collect things Mexican in an apartment on Lankershim. Most apartments were filled with trash, holding perhaps one gem that would freeze a child's interest long enough to realize the moment and its significance—perhaps a TV to sell to the local pawnshop—usually only enough stuff found to pay the back rent owed or to pay for the supplies needed to clean the dust the bodies left behind. Most things found never really mattered (because they no longer mattered to those who had long left). The people left parts of what no longer had meaning to them, things unfound, uncatalogued objects with no relationship to anyone's past.

In front of me, hundreds of shelves lined the walls—makeshift constructions; back-to-back they stood in the five-hundred-square-foot space. Shelves of books, maybe five, ten feet high, stacked three hundred per case. Cookbooks of all eras. Yearbooks from high schools never attended, the Mexican high schools in Boyle Heights, MacArthur

Park. Menus from all the taquerías in the neighborhood, dating back to when they were still written in Spanish.

To the right of me, a collection of cookery, thirty or forty *molcajetes*, five *comales*, boxes of spices for the kitchen, sat in boxes. To the left, cacti from every region, maybe fifty, some three feet tall, others three inches. At my feet, records and tapes, eight-tracks, Little Joe, Jovita G., and local bootleg tapes made—by him?—at Mexican clubs on Sepulveda.

On the table in front of me, a large platter of perfectly placed *pan dulce*, a stacked monument made from the largest *pan de huevo*, a layer of *cuernos*, of *empanadas*, of *bizcochos*, of *elotes*, of *marranitos*, of *almohadas*, topped with the smallest *pan de burro—pan dulce* finds its flavor, its origin, one hundred years earlier when Mexico meets France—in the Pastry War of 1838—followed by the second invasion in 1861 by Napoleon III, which led to the reign of Maximilian. Maximilian would begin a campaign promoting *la comida afrancesada* (Frenchified cooking). For years France affected the culture of Mexico. My aunt Peggy told me that one of my ancestors was a French colonel in the Pastry War. No one remembers the Pastry War and the origins of *pan dulce*.

And yet, in my mind the task—to dismantle indifference, to recover ash, to break down the life's work of a man who took it upon himself to document things unknown, things still unknowable. Again, I wonder: What goes first? What stays?

> *When I came to California in 1918 I was twenty-four, and I*
> *tried to find Thayer but he had moved to the East somewhere*
> *and was never heard from again; he was deemed a failure at*
> *capturing history too, I suspect; he sold pieces of the battle, for*
> *propaganda mostly, but never was able to work in Hollywood*

again; I found work cleaning at the Sepulveda library; I had no English, so I spent my nights readings kids' books, and over the years I learned how to speak, read, and write English better than most my age; I was forty by the time they let me shelve books; I still cleaned at night but once in a while someone would call in sick and they would let me do the work of a librarian. By the time I was fifty, I was the head librarian of the place; most of the old ladies had died, and I was the only one left knowing the library; the pinches still paid me what a janitor made, but I did all right; plus I had the place to myself; I must have read every book in the place, twice; I tried to get Spanish books, but the library board never let me—"We don't carry Spanish books; our patrons are English speakers and this is America after all." So I ordered every book you can find about Mexico and South America in English; I even ordered five books on Villa; all wrong; I should have written a book about our times together; maybe someday. One day, though, I will never forget: I was going through anthropology and history books about Mesoamerica and the Aztecs and that's when I found him, the father of anthropology and the inventor of the encyclopedia: Bernardino de Sahagún, a Sahagún of Sahagún and my long-lost relative; I came to know I was related to him because when I left, my grandmother told me not to give up on writing; she told me I was meant to be a man of books because I was a Sahagún, a family with a long lineage of writers; she then went on to tell me about the ancestor who started it all, Bernardino de Sahagún; she said he was a Franciscan friar who came to Mexico hundreds of years ago; I thought she was crazy because even then I knew men of the cloth did not have kids; well, I guess Sahagún had a brother who came over when he died, and he was a merchant/ soldier-for-hire for King Philip and he stayed, married an Aztec woman, and had bunches of kids; well, one of those

kids was related to me and somehow a few hundred branches
later you end up with me; well, I guess Sahagún would be my
great . . . uncle of sorts—anyhow, from that moment, I read
everything about Fray Sahagún and the Florentine Codex—
you know he never finished it. This is the important part:
I took it upon myself to write my own encyclopedia of first
the San Fernando Valley and then all things Mexican; well,
I found out that Sahagún collected everything at first, and so
this is what I began to do at the age of fifty, about the same
age that Sahagún started his own encyclopedia of the New
World; the San Fernando Valley may not be the New World
but it is a place to start, I suspect; I collected everything,
which is what you see here in the rooms, hijo—then about ten
years ago, I started writing my own encyclopedia; it's here
somewhere; but my arthritis makes it hard to write, and my
eyes are killing me these days; I will get to it again, though.
Someday. Maybe you can help me?

He had shown the encyclopedia to me once before. In a bedroom
framed by books, one locked bookcase held a facsimile copy of the
Florentine Codex. Sahagún kept it locked away with his family photos,
very few of those, and his own index, the beginnings of an encyclope-
dia, to what was held in the apartment. He put on a pair of pristine
white gloves, opened the case, and polished the leather bindings. I find
out years later that the codex was published in limited numbers in
1956 by the Mexican government, a massive four-volume tome. It sold
for over two hundred dollars in 1956; how had he been able to afford
to buy it?

Always handle the book carefully, hijo—use a book support
and respect each page—never force the bindings or pages—let
the book guide you.

Two weeks later he died. My first encounter with death would be framed with archives. It was then that I entered his archive again. The smell of death still in the room, still in the senses of my mind. I put on his gloves, too big to really fit well, and slowly took out each object and book from his cabinet. I looked at his encyclopedia first. Handwritten in English and Spanish, each item in his apartment meticulously documented and described and its origin fixed. I realize now years later, I never really left that room; I am still searching for archives and that smell of death still haunts me. Even now, I smell it in every archive I enter, this "archive fever" created from death and ash that infects and still haunts me, following me in every room I inhabit for decades after. That much I know is true.

BOOK II
Ceremonies

all writers

authenticate

I   know

They

made

truth

in these books

It was done this way.

Grammarians   employed in Ancient times

conferred many days

they,   I

explained language and I

writing the explanation

painting

lost   originals

I still have the original [documents].

EXILE (FROM TEXAS TO CALIFORNIA, 1973)

From a distance El Campo, Texas, looks as if the earth had finally swallowed it up. Seventy miles from civilization, a coastal town suffocates under the poisonous ropes of yellow-tinged hyacinths and tallow trees; the backdrop reveals smoke billowing from the nearby bay—rising, rising until the coastal breeze pushes it into the lungs of Palacios. From there, rice and cotton fields march with bodies to the edge of the parking lot, manicured earth gives way to a dilapidated American Legion dance hall called La Mangrova; on "Mexican Saturdays" we stood alone as many on the far side of town, in an undocumented sanctuary unsanctioned by the church. Smoke covers the setting sun's partial light just long enough to see the faded façade that once welcomed hundreds of documented and undocumented alike. Now layers of dust and dirt slowly eat away the siding, once smooth and red as the surrounding earth. Upon this pocked, bloodstained skin, graffiti conjoins with and mocks a mural of two dancing ghosts held in suspended relief. Deserted now by those who slowly tear down its stucco skeleton; with every passing day they learn to forget their past. No documents remain. What is left is a cracked marquee now only partially visible, specters left behind in their memory.

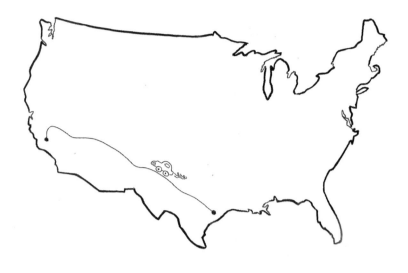

*

Lying back toward the sky, windshield framing gray heaven above, too fast to see it clear. Four years old, small enough to fit on the Malibu dashboard, a journey carried by a car colored by dusted sage, steering westward through the desert, searching. It looks like he tastes the muddy color on his lips, muted brown swirls on his puckered tongue, already starting to desensitize to Mexican flavors. His green eyes blind to their touch, overwhelmed by the vivid surroundings, for one thousand miles, terra incognita. Was this the moment he learned about panic? They wind through black asphalt roads now flecked by the dust of other travelers; their voyage to the other side of . . . now fixating on the outline of his mother's head; it looks like the broken dust has gathered in the crevices around their bodies; small mountains outline them; he embraces it; he touches the fine red-brown powder, white crystals speckled with age, like rock salt, the flavor of those mountains, of earth, of tomorrow.

CONJUNTO

Those summers I returned, I never danced, just stood listening near the stage, an outsider now, knowing no comfort in staring at their final passing; quickening thoughts of them as ghostly echoes, now finding their rhythms as silhouettes in this empty American Legion dance hall, in El Campo, Texas, 1976, erased words buried within unrelenting dreams now heard, over and over, the station music now haunting; the voyeur turns inward through sound, finally learning to embrace the melodic cacophony of now-dead voices that once surrounded him, through them. I heard others from the procession, two pulsing two-part beats, the *acordeonista* dancing with the *bajo sexto*, rising with the harmony of mourners who silence their tears with the crackling *gritos* from bodies swaying back and forth, boots clacking on the floor, touching and creating a resonating, haunting tone with lyrics that find their meaning in our loss. Even now I hear them when I close my eyes, matching the beat of a heart skipping to the beat of an anxiety created from loss.

*

I am left with sonic vibrations that form archives echoing the past.

*

Desde Laredo a San Antonio
yo he venido a casarme con mi Chencha
y no he podido por ser mojado
pues para todo me exigen la licencia
Se me hizo fácil comprar un carro
para sacar a pasear a mi Crescencia
y por la noche fui a dar al bote
porque no traía ni luces ni licencia
Al fin de todo salí del bote
con muchas ganas de ver a mi Chencha
la hallé paseando con un gabacho
el mero jefe que arregla las licencias
Ando buscando también trabajo
soy carpintero y mariachi de experiencia
de qué me sirve mi buen oficio
si para todo me exigen la licencia
Ya me regreso para Laredo

aquí he sufrido ya basta de vergüenza
estos gabachos son abusados
perdí mi carro y me quitaron a Chencha

From Laredo to San Antonio
I have come to marry my Chencha
and I could not because I'm a wetback
for everything I need a license
It was easy for me to buy a car
to take my Crescencia out on the town
and at night I ended up in jail
because I didn't have lights or a license
At the end of everything I left jail
really wanting to see my Chencha
I found her out with a *gabacho*
the very boss who arranges the licenses
I am also looking for work
I'm a carpenter and experienced mariachi
what use is my good profession
if for everything they demand a license
I'm going back to Laredo now
here I've suffered enough shame
these gabachos are abusive
I lost my car and they took my Chencha

TILE MARTYRS

Two unsolved murder mysteries remain open in Boulder: one surrounding the murder of a young girl named JonBenét Ramsey who has received hundreds of thousands of hours of news coverage, and another surrounding the murders of six young Chicanx activists who, to Chicanxs, are known as Los Seis de Boulder, the lost children of El Movimiento. Boulder and the nation have nearly been successful in erasing the bodies of Francisco Dougherty, 20; Heriberto Terán, 24; Florencio Granado, 31; Reyes Martínez, 26; Una Jaakola, 24; and Neva Romero, 21. Their cars were blown up with professionally made car bombs two days apart in the month of May 1974. Their homicides are still listed as a cold case, but Chicanxs know it was the work of the FBI. The FBI had been trying to infiltrate El Movimiento and break down its resistance. Reports state that the blasts were so powerful that pieces of their bodies were found miles away from the explosion site.

Forty-five years later in a studio on the Boulder campus, my daughter and I join dozens of activists who are attempting to reconstruct the bodies of Los Seis and build a memorial called "Los Seis de Boulder." She and I work on small colored tiles that will re-create the face of

Reyes Martínez. With each tile we attempt to piece together his dead body and resurrect it from obscurity. The ceremony is haunting. It feels like something between a celebration of community and a somber wake that I was not invited to. We all hope, perhaps in vain, that the university will allow us to resurrect the memorial by Temporary Building 1, the place on campus where one of the cars blew up, making it a sacred site and a haunting reminder of those who lost their lives here. An older woman working on the tiles says that we should be listening to their corrido. Dad, what is a corrido? The lady smiles at me and begins to hum:

Voy a cantar un corrido,
Que . . . en Colorado pasó.
Murieron los Seis de Boulder,
Dos noches en mayo,
En setenta y cuatro
Los almas de seis soldados
Seis fusilados
Seis hijos del bien

The same month that we fight for the memorialization of these young activists, John Ramsey sits down with Dr. Oz to do yet another in-depth interview about the JonBenét murder. Let me begin by saying this is such a tragedy, Dr. Oz laments. America's daughter is lost to us forever.

*

Addendum: On May 21, 2019, there was a small Los Seis ceremony at TB1 on the campus of the University of Colorado to erect the concrete memorialization of the lost ghosts of Boulder.

BOOK III
Origins

Books

empty
things

fictions

divine
rational

falsehoods

belief
idolatry

in
out

Books

ENCYCLOPEDIA

Poetry has its monsters as nature does . . . which we would fear perhaps we had made too detailed, were it not of the most fundamental importance to know well the object of an ENCYCLOPEDIA ourselves, and to expose it clearly to others.

-PRELIMINARY DISCOURSE TO THE ENCYCLOPEDIA OF DIDEROT, 1751-

Encyclopaedias trouble themselves a great deal with words fallen into disuse, never about words still unknown, burning to be uttered. The encyclopaedia worthy of its name cannot trouble itself with realistic considerations. It has a duty to remedy a deficiency.

-GEORGES BATAILLE ET AL., ENCYCLOPAEDIA DA COSTA, 1947-

Encyclopedias provide historical snapshots and are not pure; they are about knowledge, but are also rife with erasures that reveal biases in canon formation.

Encyclopedia: a form innately excessive yet orderly; a humming field; an unpredictable gathering; an antennae textual body.

-TISA BRYANT, ENCYCLOPEDIA, 2006-

Encyclopedias and the documents contained within them fight finitude and our anxious death drive, but in doing so, they do not resurrect the person as whole, but rather as partial and fleeting, a documented ghost resurrected through ashed pulp. It is not surprising that in our culture of hyperdocumentality and creative destruction, the modern print encyclopedia and those who sold it cannot escape death. Let us not forget that the encyclopedia salesman died in 2007. Throughout the Internet, a satire about Scott "Willie" Lohman, a parodic play off of Arthur Miller's Willy Loman, traveled like a virus, eulogizing the fact that he had taken his last steps for *Encyclopedia Britannica*. Wikipedia's wireless routers had finally solved one of the hardest mathematical conundrums—"the traveling salesman problem"—one of the most studied problems in computational mathematics. With the solution of the paradox by mathematicians, the last salesman died: there was no perfect profitable route a salesman could take to disseminate knowledge. Indeed, the best, most direct, shortest route was found in cyberspace, with its simulated space and digital knowledge. Wikipedia published the solution in an algorithm created by an invisible hand. The ghost in the machine emerges as the last *Homo documentator*.

Willie's death occurred despite the fact that both *World Book Encyclopedia* and *Encyclopedia Britannica*, the two largest employers of encyclopedia salesmen, neither denied nor confirmed having given up on their traveling sales divisions. For decades, the encyclopedia salesman was the main vehicle through which portable knowledge circulated in the United States. With book in hand, he traveled an area of up to two thousand square miles selling information to a mostly white emerging middle class. Ironically, the birth of the encyclopedia salesman is not documented, though his mercantile ancestors had their origins in the 1840s, when the American industrial revolution arose. The salesman was the hand that reached out to rural America, the first domestic exporter/importer. By the 1930s, conservative estimates put the number of traveling encyclopedia salesmen at three hundred thousand, though some say the numbers were near a million. But the encyclopedia salesman was a breed unto himself. He, the salesman, was almost always male and white, and he did not peddle cosmetics, vacuums, snake oil, or the other goods of capitalist desire that would help define the character of the white American middle class. The encyclopedia salesman sold the promise of white uplift through portable knowledge. *Britannica*'s mission: to have a set of encyclopedias in every home in the United States and eventually the world. By the early 1980s, 40 percent of American households found a spot in their homes for hundreds of pounds of books. And still, there is no entry in the online *Britannica* or Wikipedia or *World Book* that covers the history of the encyclopedia salesman. What will be known? Perhaps an epitaph noting that this is the moment, the point about which some historian from some future date will write: Here lies Willy Loman. Died on a humid day in June 2007.

*

Without documents I can't recall his name. So I don't remember exactly what he looked like. But I remember him like this: He wore a suit in August. I do know that he was the only salesman in one of the most Mexican-populated areas in Los Angeles County, the San Fernando Valley, North Hollywood. I do know that he was Mexican. I do not know if he was the only Mexican encyclopedia salesman in the world. I do know that he was to me. His car was a clean, brown Pinto. Though his car was well-kept, he did not drive it house to house, an act that would not be strange in L.A. No, our salesman parked his Pinto nearly a mile away. Every morning he would depart from his car and walk a route with every step perfectly planned. Like all good salesmen of his time, the night before he entered a new neighborhood he mapped out the exact route, marking meticulously the shortest and most direct path. When first seeing him from a distance, you would think he was lost or confused, or perhaps you might think he was a neighbor who was searching for a long-lost memory or a home he had once called at during his youth. He would not go door-to-door; rather, he zigzagged through the streets, sometimes only visiting one house per block. As an only child and latchkey kid, I spent hours watching him from our upstairs apartment. Every morning he would grab four volumes of the *World Book Encyclopedia*, perhaps A, E, M–N, and O, my favorite letters, and follow his route, a journey he had now planned out for nearly ten years.

He came to our green stucco house when I was ten. Our fifth rental in as many years, it stood separate from a small apartment complex of people I never knew. When the salesman knocked, I knew who he was. I had seen him for over a week, weaving his way through the neighborhood, waving to every person who approached or drove by. He passed our house four times before he knocked. Each of those times I was alone. The day he finally approached, my mother was home; he knocked. She answered the door, as if she had planned this day; her steps brisk and assured of his visit. She let him in. He did not begin selling his encyclopedia; rather, he asked if I liked my school: "You attend Toluca Lake Elementary, don't you?" His voice free of any hint of Spanish, as monotone as the brown suit he wore. "Yes," I said, "but . . . but . . ." My mother interrupted, "He skipped a grade, you know." He looked at her. He had found his way in, the focus of his sales pitch in sight—me. He continued to ask me questions about my school, what I liked about it and the subjects I found interesting. With each answer, he would refer to his books, highlight my knowledge with his meticulously documented encyclopedia. They were beautiful. Faux brown leather and gold-leaf edges, thick paper that slid like plastic silk over my forefinger. "A library at your fingertips": he repeated his slogan over and over.

My mother bought the full set and the supplemental volumes, which, he assured us, would come quarterly. Two hundred pounds and a footprint of five feet took up valuable real estate in our eight-hundred-square-foot apartment. This was the largest purchase my mother ever made. We paid in monthly installments; it took two years to pay them off. By then, however, I had lost interest. Despite the supplemental volumes, the organized knowledge in my encyclopedia slowly escaped the bindings. Despite their physical enormity, they simply could not keep up with the pace of new knowledge: every moment a new anecdote, every day a new fact, every year a revision of history would tarnish the gold leaf of the pages.

＊

I think somewhere around here I still have the dictionary. The rest of the volumes are lost, fleeting ghosts of my memory. I still can't recall his name.

EDUCATION

My education is a document of erased memory.

*

WESTMINSTER SCHOOL DIST. OF ORANGE COUNTY et al.
v. MENDEZ et al.
No. 11310

UNITED STATES CIRCUIT COURT OF APPEALS,
NINTH CIRCUIT 161 F.2d 774; 1947 U.S. App. LEXIS 2835

April 14, 1947
COUNSEL:
Joel E. Ogle, County Counsel, George F. Holden and Royal E. Hubbard, Deputies County Counsel, all of Santa Ana, Cal., for appellant.
David C. Marcus, Los Angeles, Cal. (William Strong, of Los Angeles, Cal., of counsel), for appellees.
Thurgood Marshall, and Robert L. Carter, both of New York City, and Loren Miller, of Los Angeles, Cal., for Nat. Ass'n Advancement of Colored People, amicus curiae.

Will Maslow and Pauli Murray, both of New York City, Anne H. Pollock, of Los Angeles, Cal. (Alexander H. Pekelis, of New York City, Spe. Advisor), for American Jewish Congress, amicus curiae.

Julien Cornell, Arthur Garfield Hays and Osmond K. Fraenkel, all of New York City, A. L. Wirin and Fred Okrand, both of Los Angeles, Cal., for American Civil Liberties Union, amicus curiae.

Charles F. Christopher, of Los Angeles, Cal., for Nat. Lawyers Guild, Los Angeles Chapter, amicus curiae.

A. L. Wirin and Saburo Kido, both of Los Angeles, Cal., for Japanese-American Citizens League.

Robert W. Kenney, Atty. Gen., of Cal., and T. A. Westphal, Jr., Deputy Atty. Gen., for Atty. Gen. of Cal., amicus curiae.

JUDGES: Before GARRECHT, DENMAN, MATHEWS, STEPHENS, HEALY, BONE, and ORR, Circuit Judges.

OPINION:

The petition herein which prays for present and future relief and costs is filed under authority of section 24, subdivision 14, of the Judicial Code, 28 U.S.C.A. § 41(14),[1] and section 43 of 8 U.S.C.A.,[2] and is based upon alleged violations of petitioners' civil rights as guaranteed by the 5th and 14th amendments to the Constitution of the United States. No argument as to the application of the 5th amendment is made in this appeal and it need not be considered.

The petition contains allegations to the following effect. A number of minors (at least one each from each school division herein mentioned) for themselves and for some 5000 others as to whom the allegations of the complaint apply,[3] citizens of the United States of Mexican descent, who attend the public schools of the State of California in Orange County, filed a petition by their fathers, as next friends, for relief against trustees and superintendents of several school districts and against the superintendent and secretary and **members** of a city board of education. Unless we shall indicate otherwise, our use of the terms "school districts," "districts" or "schools" will be **understood as inclusive of** both district and city school territories or schools. The term "school officials" includes all respondents.

To the petition, the school officials respond by a motion to dismiss for lack of federal court jurisdiction, because (to use the words of the motion) "this is not a suit at law or in equity authorized by law to be brought by **any person** to redress the deprivation, **under** color of any law, statutes, ordinances, regulation, custom, or usage, of any state, of any right, privilege, or immunity, secured by any law of the United States providing for equal rights of citizens of the United States or of all persons within the jurisdiction of the United States," and because the "petition fails to state a claim upon which relief can be granted." The motion was denied without prejudice to the assertion of any available legal defenses by way of answers to the petition. Respondents in their answer reassert their position as to the law in the motion to dismiss, and put in issue all of the allegations relating to the subject of segregation.[4]

After **submission** of the case for decision, the court filed its written opinion under the title "Conclusions of the Court."[4a] Thereafter, Findings of Fact and Conclusions of Law were filed, generally supporting petitioners' complaint. Respondents objected to the Findings of Fact on the ground that the evidence showed without conflict school children of Mexican descent had been and are being furnished with facilities fully equal to other school children, and that no finding had been made thereon. The court overruled the objection, and declined to make the requested finding upon the ground that it is immaterial to the issue of the case.

Thereafter, a judgment was entered to the effect that all segregation found to have been practiced was and is arbitrary and discriminating and in violation of rights guaranteed to plaintiffs by the Constitution of the United States. All respondents were enjoined against continuance of the segregation, and costs were entered against the several school districts. Respondents appeal from the judgment upon eight points which may be stated simply as contentions that the District Court was and is without jurisdiction over **the subject** matter because no substantial federal question is put in issue, and that suit is not authorized by law to redress the alleged deprivation of constitutional rights and that the findings do not support the conclusions.

Summed up in a few words it **is the burden of** the petition that the State of California has denied, and is denying, the school children of Mexican **descent**, residing in the school districts described, the equal protection of the laws of the State of California and thereby have deprived, and are **depriving,** them of their liberty and property without due process of law, as guaranteed by the Fourteenth Amendment of the Constitution of the United States.[5]

Respondents are officers of the State of California in the Department of Education of that state, and as it will hereinafter be shown their action under the intendment of the Fourteenth Amendment is the action of the state in all cases where such action is taken under **color** of state law. We must, therefore, consider the questions: Are the alleged acts done under color of state law, and do they deprive petitioners of any constitutional right? The jurisdictional question is implicit in these two questions.

It is said in Bell v. Hood, 327 U.S. 678, 682, 66 S. Ct. 773, 776, that "the court must assume jurisdiction to decide whether the allegations state a cause of action of which the court can grant relief as well as to determine issues of fact arising in the controversy." Therefore, the District Court was right in taking jurisdiction.

Were the **acts** complained of performed under color of state law, or since there is not dispute that the law of California does not authorize the segregation practiced, are the acts merely personal to the actors and in no sense state acts? That the acts complained to have been and are being performed under color of state law has been conclusively and affirmatively answered in principle in Home Telephone & Telegraph Co. v. Los Angeles, 227 U.S. 278, 33 S. Ct. 312, 57 L. Ed. 510, wherein it was claimed that the officer complained of was a state agent and the state could not be held responsible for acts of the agency not within the terms **of** the **agency. We** quote from page 287 of 227 U.S., at page 315 of 33 S. Ct., 57 L. Ed. 510 of the opinion: "In other words, the proposition is that the Amendment (Fourteenth Amendment of the Constitution) deals only with the acts of state officers within the strict scope of the public powers **possessed** by them, and does not include an abuse of power by an officer as the result of a wrong done in excess of the power delegated. Here again the settled construction of the Amendment is that it presupposes the possibility of an abuse by a state officer or representative of the powers possessed, and deals with such a contingency. It provides, therefore, for a case where one who is in possession of state power uses that power to the doing of the wrongs which the Amendment forbids, even though the consummation of the wrong may not be within the powers possessed, if the commission of the wrong itself is rendered possible or is efficiently aided by the state authority lodged in **the. wrongdoer**. That is to say, the theory of the Amendment is that where an officer or other representative of a state, in the exercise of the authority with which he is clothed, misuses **the** power **possessed** to do a wrong forbidden by the Amendment, inquiry concerning whether the state has authorized the wrong **is irrelevant** (as to the point under discussion), and the Federal judicial power is competent to afford redress for the wrong by dealing with the officer and the result of his exertion of power." See Barney v. City of New York, 193 U.S. 430, 24 S. Ct. 502, 48 L. Ed. 737; Snowden v. Hughes, 321 U.S. 1, 64 S. Ct. 397, 88 L. Ed. 497; Cochran v. Kansas, 316 U.S. 255, 62 S. Ct. 1068, 86 L. Ed. 1453.

The latest case upon the subject to which our attention has been called is Screws v. United States, 325 U.S. 91, 65 S. Ct. 1031, 89 L. Ed. 1495, 162 A.L.R. 1330. That case is a criminal one, and treats of a criminal statute implementing the Fourteenth Amendment as 8 U.S.C.A. § 43 implements the Amendment in our case. **The principles to be applied are the same.** At page 111 of 325 U.S., at page 1040 of 65 S. Ct., 89 L. Ed. 1495, 162 A.L.R. 1330 of the opinion it is said: "We are not dealing here with a case where an officer not authorized to act nevertheless takes action. Here the state officers were authorized to make an arrest and to take such steps as were necessary to make the arrest effective. They acted without authority only in the sense that they used excessive force in making the arrest effective. **It is clear that** under 'color' of law means under 'pretense' of law. Thus acts of officers in the ambit of their personal pursuits are plainly excluded. Acts of officers who undertake to perform their official duties are included whether they hew to the line of their authority or overstep it. If, as **suggested**, the statute was designed to embrace only action which the State in fact authorized, the words 'under color of any law' were hardly apt words to express the idea." See United States v. Classic, 313 U.S. 299, 61 S. Ct. 1031, 85 L. Ed. 1368, wherein the court said: "Misuse of power, possessed by virtue of state law and made possible only because the wrongdoer is clothed with the authority of state law, is action taken 'under color of state law.'"

It is clear of **doubt** that the acts complained of in the instant case pertain to the subject of the respondents' power and duties. Respondents, in immediate charge of the schools, have limited authority to receive or reject persons presenting themselves as pupils, and while acting to receive or reject, they are acting within the general scope of such authority whether the acts are right or wrong. The denial of school privileges to persons in certain schools upon the sole ground **of their ancestry** by respondents is not "in the ambit of their personal pursuits," but are acts undertaken in the performance of their official duties. However, the respondents "did not hew to the line of their authority"; they overstepped it. To the same intent are the following quotations from Home Tel. & Tel., supra, "the provisions of the Fourteenth Amendment generic in their terms are addressed, of course, to the states, **but also to every** person who is the repository of state power." At page 286 of 227 U.S., at page 314 of 33 S. Ct., 57 L. Ed. 510. "The **subject** must be **tested by** assuming that the officer possessed the power if the act be one which there would not be opportunity to perform but for **possession** of some state authority." At page 289 of 227 U.S., at page 315 of 33 S. Ct., 57 L. Ed. 510.

We hold that the respondents acting to segregate the school children as alleged in the petition were performing under color of California State law.

The court found that the segregation as alleged in the petition has been **for several years past** and is practiced under regulations, **customs** and usages **adopted** more or less as a common plan and enforced by respondent-appellants throughout the mentioned school districts; that petitioners are citizens of the United States of Mexican ancestry of good moral habits, free **from infectious** disease or any other disability, and are fully qualified to attend and use the public school facilities; that respondents occupy official positions as alleged in the petition.

In both written and oral argument our attention has been directed to the cases in which the highest court of the land has upheld state laws providing for limited segregation of the great **races of mankind**. In Roberts v. City of Boston, 5 Cush. Mass., 198,[6] a law providing for the segregation of colored school children was **held** valid in an opinion by Chief Justice Shaw of the Supreme Judicial Court of Massachusetts, but that equal facilities must be provided for the use of the colored children. Chief Justice Wallace of the Supreme Court of California in Ward v. Flood, 48 Cal. 36, 17 Am. Rep. 405, followed with approval. Cumming v. Board of Education, 175 U.S. 528, 20 S. Ct. 197, 44 L. Ed. 262, reaffirmed the principle. In Gong Lum v. Rice, 275 U.S. 78, 48 S. Ct. 91, 72 L. Ed. 172, **the principle of** the

Roberts case, supra, was followed in the opinion written by Chief Justice Taft and affirmed the State Supreme Court of Mississippi in its application of the "colored" school segregation statute to an American citizen of pure Chinese **blood.** Plessy v. Ferguson, 163 U.S. 537, 16 S. Ct. 1138, 41 L. Ed. 256, was upon the right of the state to require segregation of colored and white persons in public conveyances, and **the act** so providing was sustained again upon the principles expressed by Chief Justice Shaw. This list of cases **is by no means complete.**

It is argued by appellants that we should reverse the judgment in this case upon the authority of the segregation cases just cited because the Supreme Court has upheld the right of the states to provide for segregation upon the requirement that equal facilities be furnished each segregated group. Appellees argue that the segregation cases do not rule the instant case. There is argument in two of the amicus curiae briefs that we should strike out independently on the whole question of segregation, on the ground that recent world stirring events have set men to the reexamination of concepts considered fixed. Of course, judges as well as all others must keep abreast of the times but judges must ever be on their guard lest they rationalize outright legislation under the too free use of the power to interpret. **We are not tempted by the siren** who calls to us that the sometimes slow and tedious ways **of democratic** legislation is [*sic*] no longer respected in a progressive society. For reasons presently to be stated, we are of the opinion that the segregation cases do not rule the instant case and that is **reason** enough for not responding to the argument that we should consider them in the light of the amicus curiae briefs. In the first place we are aware of no authority justifying any segregation fiat by an administrative or executive decree as every case cited to us is based upon a legislative act. The segregation in this case is without legislative support and comes into fatal collision with the legislation of the state.

The State of California has a state-wide free school system governed by general law, the local application of which by necessity is to a considerable extent, under the direction of district and city school boards or trustees, superintendents and teachers.

Section 16601 of the California Educational Code requires the parent of any child between the ages of eight and sixteen years to send him to the full time day school. There are some few exceptions, but none of them are pertinent here. There are no exceptions based upon the ancestry of the child other than those contained in Secs. 8003, 8004, Calif.Ed.C. (both repealed as of 90 days after June 14, 1947), which includes Indians under certain conditions and children of Chinese, Japanese or Mongolian parentage. As to these, there are laws requiring them in certain cases to attend separate schools. Expressio Unius Est Exclusio Alterius. It may appropriately be noted that the segregation so provided for and the segregation referred to in the cited cases includes only children of parents belonging to one or another of **the** great **races of mankind**.[7] It is interesting to note at this juncture of the case that the parties stipulated that there is no **question** as to race segregation in the case. Amicus curiae brief writers, however, do not agree that this is so. Nowhere in any California law is there a suggestion that any segregation can be made of children within one of the great races. Thus it is seen that there is a substantial difference in our case from those which have been decided by the Supreme Court, a difference which possibly could be held as placing our case outside the scope of such decisions. However, we are not put to this choice as the state law permits of segregation only as we have stated, that is, it is definitely confined to Indians and certain named Asiatics. That the California law does not include the segregation of school children because of **their blood,** is definitely and **affirmatively** indicated as the trial judge pointed out, by the fact that legislative action has been **taken** by the State of California to admit to her schools, children citizens of a foreign country, living **across the border**. Calif.Ed.C. §§ 16004, 16005. Mexico is the only foreign country on any California boundary.[8]

It follows that the acts of respondents were and are entirely without authority of California law, notwithstanding their performance has been and is under color or pretense of California law. Therefore, conceding for the argument that California could legally enact a law authorizing the segregation as practiced, the fact stands out unchallengeable that California has not done so but to the contrary has enacted laws wholly inconsistent with such practice. By enforcing the segregation of school children of Mexican descent against their will and contrary to the laws of California, respondents have violated the federal law as provided in the Fourteenth Amendment to the Federal Constitution by depriving them **of liberty** and property without due process of law and by denying to them the equal protection of the laws.

It may be said at this point that the practice could be stopped through the application of California law in California State Courts, and this may be so but the idea is of no relevancy. Mr. Justice Douglas made this point clear in the case of Screws v. United States, supra, when he said that the Fourteenth Amendment does not come into play merely because the federal law or the state law under which the officer purports to act is violated. *"It is applicable when and only when some one is deprived of a federal right by that action."* (Emphasis ours.) And it is as appropriate for us to say here, what Mr. Justice Douglas said in a like situation in the cited case, "**We agree** that when this statute is applied (in our case when Sec. 41(14) of 28 U.S.C.A. is applied) it should be construed so as to respect the proper balance between the states and the federal government in law enforcement." Punishment for the act would be legal under either or both federal and state governments. United States v. Lanza, 260 U.S. 377, S. Ct. 103, 71 L. Ed. 270, 48 A.L.R. 1102. However, since the practice complained of has continued **for several consecutive years,** apparent to California executive and peace officers, and continues, it cannot be said that petitioners violated Mr. Justice Douglas' admonition in taking their action in a federal court.

In the view of the case we have herein taken the contention that the Findings of Fact do not support the Conclusions of Law and the Judgment is wholly unmeritorious. The pleadings, findings and judgment in this case refer to children of "Mexican and Latin descent and extraction," but it does not appear that any segregation of school children other than those of Mexican descent was practiced. Therefore, we have confined our comment thereto. If the segregation of all children of Latin descent and extraction in addition to those of Mexican descent were included in the practice and the plan, its illegality would, of course, be upon the same basis as that herein found. In addition, however, the impossibility of there being any reason for the inclusion in the segregation plan of all children of Latin descent and extraction and **the palpable** impossibility of its enforcement would brand any such plan **void on its face.**[9]

> Affirmed.
>
> *DENMAN, Circuit Judge*
> *(concurring).*

I concur in what is said in the court's opinion but cannot agree with the omission of the consideration of Lopez v. Seccombe, so widely discussed in the profession. **I am** also of the opinion that we should not place a primary reliance upon Home Telephone & Telegraph Co. v. Los Angeles, which in particulars relevant here is overruled by the Snowden and Screws cases. The precedent of the recent decision in Snowden v. Hughes, infra, states the law as it now is, with requirements for violation of the Fourteenth Amendment not mentioned in the court's opinion.

(1) Lopez v. Seccombe, Mayor of the City of San Bernardino, California, D.C., S.D.Cal., 71 F. Supp. 769.

What our decision here does is to follow the precedent of Judge Yankwich's decision in the Lopez case. It is not only in Orange County that public officers are guilty of such perversions of the "privileges long recognized at common law as essential to the orderly pursuit of happiness by free men."[1] In an adjoining county a similar discrimination was made not only against **the descendants** of Mexican nationals but **of descendants**, adult and infant, of all nationals of Latin countries.

San Bernardino established a public park and recreational ground with an area containing a swimming pool and bath house. The mayor, city councilmen, chief of police and park superintendent, all through their agents, **barred** from their entry into the area all persons **of** *Latin* **descent**. The exclusion was not merely of Mexicans but of all Latins, that is **of people** from the score or more Latin American Republics and from Italy, Spain and Portugal, as the outstanding character of persons actually **excluded** makes clear.

The Reverend R. N. Nunez is a **Catholic** priest of Mexican **ancestry**. Eugenio Nogueros is from Porto Rico, of Latin ancestry, a college graduate, who **is an editor** and publisher. Ignacio Lopez, another newspaper editor, is **of** Mexican **descent**, a graduate of the University of California, recently the head of the Spanish Department in the Office of Foreign Language, Division of Office of War Information, and the Spanish speaking director of the Office of Coordinator of Inter-American Affairs at Los Angeles, California. All are citizens of the United States. The two editors were taxpayers contributing to the support of the facilities denied them.

All three sought admission to the park area and its facilities and were excluded therefrom because of their Latin descent. **This** was not a mere casual **error of** a minor official at the park. **The priest** and the two editors and each of them on several occasions protested *to these city officials* and requested their permission to enter these public facilities but, because of their Latin descent, such permission was **denied** them.

In the case of Lopez et al. v. Seccombe et al., supra, the priest and the two editors, suing for themselves as

American citizens and *eight thousand* (8,000) other San Bernardino persons of Latin **descent**, sought an injunction against the mayor, councilmen, chief of police and park superintendent for such discriminatory exclusion. **The** case was tried by Judge Yankwich who ruled, as the instant case, that such discriminatory barring of the class of Latin **descended people violated** the due process and equal protection clause of the Fourteenth Amendment. The facts of the discrimination as to **all persons of Latin descent** were found, as above stated, and an injunction issued against the eight office holders.

In **the** San Bernardino case the answer of the officers denied the exclusion of the plaintiffs. In the instant case these Orange County trustees, **public** officers sworn to uphold the Constitution of the United States and the constitution of the State of California,[2] brazenly **proclaim their guilt** in their discriminatory violation of the state educational laws. What is **overlooked** in the court's opinion is the fact that the appellants themselves declare they have violated **their oaths** of office and, in effect, say, "Well what are you going to do about it?" for their brief states

"The situation in California as conclusively shown by the record is:

"1. The legislative department of the State has clearly and expressly prohibited the establishment of separate schools for Mexican pupils.

"2. The Judicial Department of the State has emphatically declared it to be unlawful to establish separate schools for Mexican pupils (Wysinger v. Crookshank, 82 Cal. 588, 23 P. 54)."

California is a state as large as France and having a population at least a fifth as large as that of the United States when the Fourteenth Amendment was adopted. All the nations of the world have contributed to its people. Were the vicious principle sought to be established in Orange and San Bernardino Counties followed elsewhere, in scores of school districts the adolescent minds of American children would **become infected.** To the wine producing valleys and hills of northern counties emigrated thousands of Italians whose now third generation descendants well could have their law-breaking school officials segregate **the descendants** of the north European nationals.

Likewise in the raisin districts of the San Joaquin Valley to which came the thousands of Armenians who have contributed to national prominence such figures as Saroyan and Haig Patigan. So in the coastal town homes of fishermen, largely from the Mediterranean nations, **the historic antipathies** of Italian, Greek and Dalmatian nationals could be injected and perpetuated in their citizen school children.

Or, to go to **the descendants** of an ancient Mesopotamian nation, whose facial characteristics **still survived** in the inspiring beauty of Brandeis and Cardozo **the descendants** of the nationals of Palestine, among whose people later began our so-called Christian civilization, as well could be segregated and Hitler's anti-semitism have a long start in the country **which gave** its youth to **aid in its destruction.**

It is to such school officials, **who so violate their oaths** of office and openly break both the state and federal laws and who set such an example **to the boys and girls**, that these adolescents are **entrusted** to grow up in the American way of life. In this connection it should be noted that Section 19 of the Criminal Code, 18 U.S.C.A. § 51, under which Screws was prosecuted, makes a felony of the same wrongdoing for which the succeeding Section 20, 18 U.S.C.A. § 52, creates the civil remedy here given by this court. As justice Rutledge's opinion at page 119 of 325 U.S., at page 1044 of 65 S. Ct., 89 L. Ed. 1495, 162 A.L.R. 1330, of the Screws case states, they are "twin sections," in which there are "no differences in the basic rights guarded."

It is in accord with the long established precedent of Anglo Saxon judges to call to the attention of the prosecuting authorities facts appearing in litigation **before them** which may warrant the consideration of an indictment. Following that custom, the attention of the senior judge of the Southern District of California and the foremen of its grand juries is directed to the facts here disclosed.

(2) As the law is today it is not enough that a state official violates the state of federal law in the manner described in Home Telephone & Telegraph Co. v. Los Angeles, 227 U.S. 278, 282, 33 S. Ct. 312, 57 L. Ed. 510, to bring him within the due process and equal protection clause of the Fourteenth Amendment. On the facts shown in the opinion of the Supreme Court the City of Los Angeles today would not be held to have violated that Amendment. In Snowden v. Hughes, 321 U.S. 1, 64 S. Ct. 397, 401, 88 L. Ed. 497, the Supreme Court determined **the boundary line** of cases of officials' violations **of** state **law** within and without the Fourteenth Amendment. It is not enough that the federal or state law is violated. In addition either the law must be not "fair on its face" or there must be an "intentional or purposeful discriminatory design to favor one individual or

class over another" in administering the law. There, where an Illinois election board, in claimed violation of Illinois law, had failed to certify a citizen as a duly elected nominee for a state office, it was held that he was not **denied** the equal protection of the Fourteenth Amendment. This was not because he had a remedy under the state law but because that law was not discriminatory on **its face** and there was no **showing** of the board's intentional or purposeful discrimination of a "particular class." In holding the Amendment not violated, the Court, at page 8 of 321 U.S., at page 401 of 64 S. Ct., 88 L. Ed. 497, states the distinction between a mere incidental violation of a non-discriminatory state law and a purposeful "class" discrimination, as follows:

"The unlawful administration by state officers of a *state statute fair on its face*, resulting in its unequal application to those who are entitled to be treated alike, is not **a denial** of equal protection *unless there is shown to be present in it an element of intentional or purposeful discrimination*. This may appear *on the face of the action taken with respect to a particular class or person*, cf. McFarland v. American Sugar Refining Co., 241 U.S. 79, 86, 87, 36 S. Ct. 498, 501, 60 L. Ed. 899, or it may only be shown by extrinsic evidence showing a discriminatory design to favor one individual or class over another not to be inferred from the action itself, Yick Wo v. Hopkins, 118 U.S. 356, 373, 374, 6 S. Ct. 1064, 1072, 1073, 30 L. Ed. 220." (Emphasis supplied.)

In the Los Angeles telephone case the sole finding of fact was that the city authorities had established a telephone rate which was confiscatory. On this alone **it** was held that the city violated the Fourteenth Amendment. There could be no finding that the law authorizing the rate fixing was not "fair on its face." Nor was there any finding of the city's purposeful discriminatory design to favor one individual or class over another.

Screws v. United States, 325 U.S. 91, 103, 65 S. Ct. 1031, 89 L. Ed. 1495, 162 A.L.R. 1330, **upholds the validity of** the twin section 19 of the Criminal Code against the charge of a **vagueness** so complete that it fails **to describe** a crime, by construing it to apply only where (at page 107 of 325 U.S., at page 1038 of 65 S. Ct.) the parties charged "had the purpose to deprive the prisoner of a constitutional right," there "the right to be tried by a court rather than by ordeal." "For the specific intent required by the Act is an intent to deprive **a person** of a right which has been made specific either by the express terms of the Constitution or laws of the United States or by decisions interpreting them." Page 104 of 325 U.S., at page 1037 of 65 S. Ct.

In three respects the instant case is even stronger than the Screws case. There the killing of the prisoner was held no more than a possible violation of the Fourteenth Amendment and punishable in the federal courts though also punishable under the state law. There the law under which the arrest was made was **"fair on its face"** and the case was returned to the jury to be tried under a proper instruction as to whether the "intent" with which the killing was committed was **to violate** that Amendment. **Here** the regulation shows **"on its face"** the denial of equal protection of the California laws, prevention of which is the very purpose of that Amendment. Here the "intent" so to deny such protection by the enforcement of the regulation is proclaimed in the briefs to this court.

*

(3) Since the applicable criterion is whether the segregating regulation of each district is discriminatory and not fair on its face, it is pertinent that they clearly fail even to give equal facilities to the children in the two classes of schools.

The teacher of a class of both English and non-English speaking pupils is not the same facility to the **English** speaking pupils that the same teacher would be to a class made up entirely of those speaking English. There is **diverted** to the teaching of English to the **Spanish** speaking pupils much of the teacher's professional energy and time which otherwise would be given to an **English speaking** class. The district court inferentially so holds in its finding XI, "**English** language deficiencies of *some* of the children of Mexican **ancestry** as such children enter elementary public school life as beginners may justify differentiation by public school authorities in the **exercise** of their reasonable discretion as to the pedagogical methods of instruction to be pursued with different pupils, and foreign **language** handicaps may be **to such a degree** in the pupils in elementary schools **as to require** separate treatment in separate classrooms. Omnibus segregation of children of Mexican ancestry from **the rest of the** student **body** in the elementary grades in the schools involved in this action because of language handicaps is not warranted by the **record** before us." (Emphasis supplied.) This court judicially is aware that a century ago when California was taken over by the United States, the majority of its population was Mexican. Four generations of these people have been educated in English speaking schools. To these should be added the third and second **generations of**

succeeding Mexican immigrants to California. A very large percentage of the present day school children descended from Mexican nationals is English speaking. Many of those of older established families do not speak Spanish. All such children are discriminated against by the impaired facility of the teacher, occupied with teaching English to their classroom associates—as compared with those attending schools of English **speaking pupils.**

NOTES

[1] Section 41. (Judicial Code, section 24, amended.) Original jurisdiction. The district courts shall have original jurisdiction as follows: (14) "Suits to redress deprivation of civil rights. Fourteenth. Of all suits at law or in equity authorized by law to be brought by any person to redress the deprivation, under color of any law, statute, ordinance, regulation, custom, or usage, of any State, of any right, privilege, or immunities, secured by the Constitution of the United States, or of any right secured by any law of the United States providing for equal rights of citizens of the United States, or of all persons within the jurisdiction of the United States."

[2] "§ 43. Civil action for deprivation of rights

"**Every** person who, under color of any statute, ordinance, regulation, custom, or usage, of any State or Territory, subjects, or causes to be subjected, any citizen of the United States or other person within the jurisdiction thereof to the deprivation of any rights, privileges, or immunities secured by the Constitution and laws, shall be liable to the party injured in an action at law, suit in equity, or other proper proceeding for redress."

[3] Rule 23 of Federal Rules of Civil Procedure, 28 U.S.C.A. following section 723c as to class suits.

[4] It is **alleged** in the answer that a large number of school **child**ren concerned are unfamiliar with and unable to speak the English language. Other affirmative defenses are alleged but they need not be mentioned for the reason that the findings of fact are not attacked and the appeal is based upon the question as to whether or not petitioners' civil rights under the Fourteenth Amendment to the Constitution of the United States **have been violated.**

[4a] **The author** of this opinion deems it appropriate to note that the case was tried to the distinguished Senior Judge of the Southern District of California, Honorable Paul J. McCormick.

[5] As to the protection and deprivation of liberty and property without due process of law clauses of the Fourteenth Amendment, see Plessy v. Ferguson, 163 U.S. 537, 547, 16 S. Ct. 1138, 41 L. Ed. 256; Bell's Gap. R. R. v. Pennsylvania, 134 U.S. 232, 10 S. Ct. 533, 33 L. Ed. 892; Missouri v. Lewis, 101 U.S. 22, 31, 25 L. Ed. 989. We quote from American Sugar Refining Co. v. Louisiana, 179 U. S. 89, 92, 21 S. Ct. 43, 44, 45 L. Ed. 102: "The act **in question** does undoubtedly discriminate in favor of a certain class of refiners, but this discrimination, if founded upon a reasonable distinction in principle, **is** valid. Of course, if such discrimination were purely arbitrary, oppressive, or **capricious**, and made to depend upon differences of color, race, nativity, religious opinions, political affiliations, or other considerations having no possible connection with the duties of citizens as taxpayers, such exemption would

be pure favoritism, and a denial of the equal protection of the laws to the less favored classes." And in Truax v. Raich, 239 U.S. 33, 41, 36 S. Ct. 7, 10, 60 L. Ed. 131, L.R.A. 1916D, 545, Ann. Cas. 1917B, 283, Mr. Justice Hughes, as an associate justice, speaking for the court said: "It is sought to justify this act [an act limiting employment of aliens] as an exercise of the power of the state to make reasonable classifications in legislating to promote the health, safety, morals, and welfare of those within its jurisdiction. But **this admitted authority**, with the broad range of legislative discretion that it implies, does not go so far as to make it possible for the state **to deny** to lawful inhabitants, because of their race or nationality, the ordinary means of earning a livelihood. It requires no argument to show that the right to work for a living in the common occupations of the community is of **the very essence** of the personal freedom and opportunity that it was the purpose of the Amendment to secure. [Cases cited.] If this could be refused solely upon the ground of race or nationality, the prohibition **of the denial** to any person of the equal protection of the laws would be a barren form of words." Meyer v. Nebraska, 262 U. S. 390, 399, 43 S. Ct. 625, 67 L. Ed. 1042, 29 A.L.R. 1446: "'No state shall deprive any person of life, liberty, or property, without due process of law.' [Fourteenth Amendment.] While this Court has not attempted to define with exactness the liberty thus guaranteed, the term has received much consideration and some of the included things have been definitely stated. Without doubt, it denotes not merely freedom from bodily restraint but also the right of the individual to contract, to engage in any of the common occupations of life, to acquire useful knowledge, to marry, establish a home and bring up children, **to worship God** according to the **dictates** of his own conscience, and generally to enjoy those privileges long recognized at common law as essential to **the** orderly **pursuit of** happiness by free men." Following this portion of the Meyer case are cases cited: In re Slaughter-House Cases, 16 Wall. 36, 21 L. Ed. 394; Butchers' Union Slaughter-House Co. v. Crescent City Live-Stock Landing Co., 111 U.S. 746, 4 S. Ct. 652, 28 L. Ed. 585; Yick Wo v. Hopkins, 118 U.S. 356, 6 S. Ct. 1064, 30 L. Ed. 220; Minnesota v. Barber, 136 U.S. 313, 10 S. Ct. 862, 34 L. Ed. 455; Allgeyer v. Louisiana, 165 U.S. 578, 17 S. Ct. 427, 41 L. Ed. 832; Lochner v. New York, 198 U.S. 45, 25 S. Ct. 539, 49 L. Ed. 937, 3 Ann.Cas. 1133; Twining v. New Jersey, 211 U.S. 78, 29 S. Ct. 14, 53 L. Ed. 97; Chicago, Burlington & Quincy R. R. Co. v. McGuire, 219 U.S. 549, 31 S. Ct. 259, 55 L. Ed. 328; Truax v. Raich, 239 U.S. 33, 38 S. Ct. 337, 62 L. Ed. 772, Ann.Cas. 1918E, 593; Adams v. Tanner, 244 U.S. 590, 37 S. Ct. 662, 61 L. Ed. 1336, L.R.A. 1917F, 1163, Ann.Cas. 1917D, 973; New York **Life** Ins. Co. v. Dodge, 246 U.S. 357, 38 S. Ct. 337, 62 L. Ed. 772, Ann.Cas. 1918E, 593; Truax v. Corrigan, 257 U.S. 312, 42 S. Ct. 124, 66 L. Ed. 254, 27 A.L.R. 375; Adkins v. Children's Hospital, 261 U.S. 525, 43 S .Ct. 394, 67 L. Ed. 785, 24 A.L.R. 1238; Wyeth v. Cambridge Board of Health, 200 Mass. 474, 86 N.E. 925, 23 L.R.A., N.S. 147, 128 Am.St.Rep. 439. See also, Farrington v. Tokushige, 273 U.S. 284, 47 S. Ct. 406, 71 L. Ed. 646; and Pierce v. Society of Sisters, 268 U. S. 510, 535, 45 S. Ct. 571, 69 L. Ed. 1070, 39 A.L.R. 468. See exhaustive discussion in Wysinger v. Crookshank, 82 Cal. 588, 23 P. 54.

[6] The decision in the case of Roberts v. City of Boston, 5 Cush. 198, cited in the majority opinion in the above entitled case (April 14, 1947), was not founded directly upon a

state statute. A state statute granted certain discretionary powers to an elected School Committee, but these powers did not specifically provide for any segregation of school children on the basis of race or color. However, Boston had long conducted separate schools for colored school children. Shortly before institution of the case (the case antedated the Civil War), which was for damages allegedly suffered by the plaintiff, a colored child; for being excluded from the school nearest her residence, the School Committee had adopted a resolution approving the policy of continuing the separate schools. The decision in the case upheld the acts of the Committee. (Stephens, C. J.)

[7] Somewhat empirically, it used to be taught that mankind was made up of white, brown, yellow, black and red men. **Such divisional designation** has little or no adherents among anthropologists or ethnic scientists. A more scholarly nomenclature is Caucasoid, Mongoloid and Negroid, yet this is unsatisfactory, as an attempt to collectively sort all mankind into distinct groups.

[8] The right of children to attend schools organized under laws of the state has been termed a fundamental right. See Wysinger v. Crookshank, 82 Cal. 588, 23 P. 54. Education "is a privilege granted by the state constitution, and is a legal right as much as is a vested right in property." 23 Cal.Jur. pp. 141, 142. In the same volume, p. 161: "It is now settled that it is not in violation of the organic law of the state or of the nation to **require** children in whom racial differences exist to attend separate schools, provided the schools are equal in every substantial respect. But only in the event such schools are established may children be separated in respect of race. And no separation

may be had, in **the absence** of statutory or constitutional authority therefor."

[9] The case of Lopez v. Seccombe, D.C. S.D.Ca., 71 F. Supp. 769, cited and commented upon in the concurring opinion, went to uncontested judgment upon stipulation, and is supported alone by formal findings **of** facts and conclusions of law. No discussion of principles appears in the record, no opinion or memorandum was filed, and no counsel in the instant case mentioned it in his brief, notwithstanding the same lawyer was chief counsel in both cases. (Stephens, C. J.)

[1] "While this Court has not attempted to define with exactness the **liberty** thus guaranteed [by due process clause of the Fourteenth Amendment], **the term** has received much consideration and some of the included things have been definitely stated. Without **doubt,** it **denotes** not merely freedom from bodily restraint but also the right of the individual [1] to contract, [2] to engage in any of the common occupations of life, [3] to acquire useful knowledge, [4] to marry, [5] to establish a home and bring up children, [6] to worship **God** according to the dictates of **his** own **conscience,** and generally to enjoy those privileges long recognized at common law as essential to the orderly pursuit of happiness by free men. — [Citing cases.]" Meyer v. Nebraska, 262 U.S. 390, 399, 43 S. Ct. 625, 626, 67 L. Ed. 1042, 29 A.L.R. 1446, holding a law prohibiting the teaching of foreign languages in school **violates** the Fourteenth Amendment.

[2] "**I** do solemnly swear (or **affirm,** as the case may be) that **I** will **support** the Constitution of the United States and the

Constitution of the State of California, and that I will **faith-fully** discharge the duties of the office of **forgive him**

*

Enough of this complicity in degradation which welds the generations, one with another; enough of tacit understandings, of shameful solutions, of a rendezvous fixed for ultimate common ruination. Enough of this long-term speculation, of this old-age pension-scheme that goes by the name of education. Cease to address, by way of the child that confronts you, the humiliated and degraded man he must finally become. Enough of this "You'll understand later on," and "When you're grown-up," to the person [in] whose eyes, at this very moment, and irremediably, you are degrading yourself.

-GEORGES BATAILLE ET AL., *ENCYCLOPAEDIA DA COSTA*, 1947-

The widespread lynching of Mexicans after the Mexican-American War, and corporeal punishment in U.S. schools well into the mid-twentieth century, compelled Mexican families to adopt English as a means of communication.

-CRISTINA RIVERA GARZA, *THE RESTLESS DEAD*-

One generation after *Mendez v. Westminster*, I become a student at Toluca Lake Elementary School in North Hollywood, part of the Los Angeles Unified School District, miles away from the school district at the heart of *Mendez v. Westminster*. Coming from Texas and having a lisp when I get nervous, I am told that I need to report to the speech bus to "check my English." I am put on the bus with ten or eleven other Mexican-surnamed first graders. I speak fluent English, not a whisper of Spanish (my dad forbade me to learn it, but that is another story);

and yet I am segregated from day one. One day turns into a week, wherein daily I am taken to a hot bus that smells of melting plastic in the middle of the parking lot where I am asked to read a book, a small hardbound document with onionskin paper and large-font letters, into a tape recorder. "Slowly, faster, slower, faster." "Enunciate." I stare at Mr. Forone and wonder what that word "annunciate" means, so I yell into the microphone, "A, apple, B, ball, C, cat . . ." They make a tape and file it under "Rivera, Texas Transfer, Race: Mexican." I am documented and for the first time I now know what I am, a Mexican. A Mexican from Texas with a lisp who does not speak Spanish. Voices fill the noxious air of the bus, one on top of another: "He does not have an accent like the others." "Just a speech impediment." "At least they taught him how to read." "Put him in Mrs. Getz's room." "That is where the others are going this year." Welcome to Los Angeles.

LA BREA'S GHOST

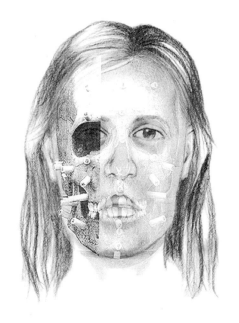

I encountered my first ghost when I was twelve. It was on a school field trip to the La Brea Tar Pits. Once a Mexican land grant, before the Treaty of Guadalupe Hidalgo of 1848, Rancho La Brea is where I found La Brea Woman, the only human to be recovered from what are now named the La Brea Tar Pits. A young woman, believed to be between eighteen and twenty-five years old, La Brea Woman lived around nine thousand years ago. Exhumed from the tar in 1914, her remains consist of a cranium, a mandible, and postcranial fragments recovered from Pit 10. The guide tells us she was murdered, with "a fractured skull and broken jaw resulting from a hit from a blunt object. The exhibit was very expensive, look how lifelike it is." I stare at the life-sized specter of her body. She is in a light-box display that creates a phantasmic hologram, highlighting her upright skeleton; with the use of special-effects lighting, artificial muscles, skin, and hair appear on her bones to reveal what she looked like in life. Her death chamber shines in my mind's eye in perpetuity.

Thirty-five years later I still see the stereoscopic specter. I wonder now . . . was she the first victim of an undocumented act of misogyny? Curated femicide haunts forever. I return in 2015 only to find out that the exhibit was removed around 2004. The director of the museum, John Harris, feared retribution from Mexicans and Native American activists, who may want her remains, and who desire to declare the pits a sacred burial ground and resurrect the Native and Mexican past of Rancho La Brea. Some believed there were more Native bodies buried in the tar pits that the museum was hiding. La Brea Woman is now entombed in a large paper box in an out-of-sight storage unit, a documented ghost far too material, far too visible, for a city that buries its Native and Mexican past in cast celluloid.

BOOK IV
Soothsayers

Birth

Foretells

NECROMANTIC

Books

9/11

To the Unknown Migrant—9/11 Memorial.

-THE 9/11 MEMORIAL, NEW YORK, NY, 2012-

*

They are still searching for the remains of the undocumented Latinx bodies nearly two decades after 9/11. The documented are officially known in Wikipedia:

The September 11 attacks *(also referred to as 9/11) were a series of four coordinated terrorist by the Islamic terrorist group al-Qaeda against the United States on the morning of Tuesday, September 11, 2001. The attacks killed 2,996 people, injured over 6,000 others, and caused at least $10 billion in infrastructure and property damage. Additional people died of 9/11-related cancer and respiratory diseases in the months and years following the attacks.*

I try to edit the entry and add the picture from the art exhibit *To the Unknown Migrant*; these are attempts to inscribe the undocumented immigrants who both died on 9/11 and continue to lose their lives cleaning up the wreckage. I edit it weekly under my Wikipedia name, La Memoria, only to have it erased seven times over seven weeks:

There are an estimated 400 unknown undocumented Latinx immigrants who worked in the World Trade Center who, true to their classification, remain undocumented, not counted in the official number of dead or memorialized. Thousands of undocumented immigrants worked cleaning up the debris only to be deported and denied promised green cards for work that would lead to their deaths decades after 9/11. Many undocumented are deported after reporting illnesses that developed after their work on the cleanup. There is a tomb under Freedom Tower, a necropolis under New York City, that holds the remains of the dead, "in perpetuity," many of whom are undocumented Latinx immigrants. Their DNA cannot be matched because there was no record of it. They will remain unknown in the tomb for eternity, in a state of purgatory under the 9/11 memorial.

APOCALYPSE 2012

The annals form served the Aztecs as one of the first methods of recording the Spanish conquest. Written secretly in 1524 by seven anonymous Aztec poets, the *Anales de Tlatelolco* chronicle the first contact with Spanish colonizers, the coming apocalypse of colonization, and the Aztec departure from Aztlán. Sahagún began compiling his tomb in Tlatelolco, and it is believed that these dissident poets worked with him on his *Florentine Codex*, burying their own chronicles under the eye of Sahagún and his Christian hand. Under the scholia of the *Florentine Codex* are their annals, some still exposed in the sectioned scholia of the codex, others erased, their apocalyptic prophecies lost in the pigment, their voices anxiously searching for a reader, now buried deep in the archives of Paris's National Library.

*

Now is the age of anxiety.

-W. H. AUDEN-

JANUARY 1, 2012 – "Did the Maya Predict World Would End in 2012?" *CBC.ca*

JANUARY 2, 2012 – *I am an archivist, but finding the exact trigger of a yearlong panic attack leaves me searching for partial and fleeting documents as if I am living in Borges's Library of Babel. I think it was today, the day I entered this archon of ash unknowingly. The day I drove under a crumbling cement bridge on Sheridan Avenue in Denver, Colorado. In that moment beneath the bridge, for some reason still unknown to me today, my mind races toward my death. I flip to another thought; I search for a radio station to distract, but my death—when will it be, how will it be, will I suffer?—keeps taking over all thoughts. Thoughts of my death flip through my mind like an old Kodak Carousel full of slides, spinning uncontrollably, revealing all parts of my inner fears with each image. The images in my mind take over my body; my heart races, flipping and skipping. I can't catch my breath; my body begins to sweat through my clothes. My mouth is so dry I can feel the white-caked saliva form on the corners of my lips. I recover, slowly, as I continue to drive, thinking that this festering feeling, this pain, must be an anomaly, but, like an unread archive, you really don't know its meaning for some time after the initial res-urrection. I search for an unknown cause, a moment, a documented time in my life, a trigger, among a world that documents everything but my ailing mind. I still find myself searching for the buried instances that triggered this yearlong panic attack, this fight with death, and like Tomás Rivera's unnamed boy hidden under the house in his novel . . . and the earth did not devour him, I too turn to documenting this lost year of anxiety.*

JANUARY 7, 2012 –

JANUARY 17, 2012 –

JANUARY 31, 2012 – "Dying Immigrant Denied Kidney Transplant Because He Is Undocumented." *ThinkProgress*

FEBRUARY 3, 2012 – "Undocumented Young Activists Talk About Depression and Suicide." *Huffington Post*

FEBRUARY 5, 2012 – *I lie in bed all day. Exhausted. I stare at the TV, search for shows without commercials about prescription drugs and diseases and their unintended side effects that will remind me of my own mortality. I can never find the right channel, but I keep searching, searching for a place without simulated patients taking drugs for scripted diseases. Why can't I get out of bed, why now? Was it my emergency appendectomy a few months prior? Could I really have died? Did the anesthesia affect my brain? I look for documentation of the surgery. I call the doctors. No one gives me an answer that resolves my worries. There are not enough channels. My body seems to trigger this anxious feeling in my mind. Everyone, every thought, everything leads me back to my body. Thoughts of my dead body, my heart stopping, cancer, heart disease, ALS, everything causes panic in my mind. I hate my body.*

MARCH 3, 2012 – "Imagine a Day Without a Mexican." *CNN*

MARCH 15, 2012 – *I escape my bed and go and watch the movie* The Age of Anxiety. *I want to learn about this condition that every news cycle seems to say is emblematic of our era. 2012 is the "Age of Anxiety," reporters say. We all feel anxiety at new levels, doctors tell us. It is very stressful to live today. We all hang on their every word, hoping they will tell us there is a cure, but they return to prescribing pills. "You can only treat anxiety. You cannot cure it." "But you are not alone. Millions have anxiety disorder." I find no comfort in knowing that others are going through this pain, going through the effects of an incurable disease. I never get comfort from others' pain, and I do not feel some special collectivity knowing others panic and worry for no reason. I think I am alone in the theater, trying to ignore the anxiety I brought with me. The seats are full of my doppelgangers, ghosts watching without a word.*

MARCH 29, 2012 – "Supreme Court Flooded with Briefs Opposing SB-1070 (Show Me Your Papers Law)." *CNN*

APRIL 1, 2012 –

APRIL 4, 2012 – "Arizona's 'Show Me Your Papers' Law in the U.S. Supreme Court: What's at Stake?" *American Progress*

APRIL 12, 2012 – "México Sube a Internet Los Códices de Fray Bernardino de Sahagún." *Vanguardia*

MAY 1, 2012 – "One in Seven Thinks the End of the World Is Coming." *Reuters*

MAY 2, 2012 – *A small part of me wants the world to end. But I want my daughter, my wife, my friends, to live. Is anxiety what the apocalypse feels like? Maybe the Age of Anxiety is the condition of living in an apocalypse that doesn't end. Yes, that is the apocalypse, a self-fulfilling end of days replicated in my mind's eye over and over. I look for a pill filled with my ash that will cure the apocalypse.*

MAY 4, 2012 – "Mayan Calendar: According to Poll One in 10 Believe That the End of the Mayan Calendar Points to Doomsday." *Huffington Post*

MAY 14, 2012 – "FDA Approves Generic Lexapro for Depression, Anxiety." *PsychCentral*

MAY 26, 2012 – "Apocalypse-Proof Condos Already Sold Out." *C/NET*

MAY 31, 2012 –

JUNE 7, 2012 – "Arizona Sheriff Joe Arpaio Arrests 6-Year-Old Undocumented Immigrant." *Huffington Post*

JUNE 8, 2012 – *I wake up and I am not nervous; I am not worrying about things I cannot control. I was told when I was young that I worry too much. They say anxiety is triggered by worrying about future events that you cannot control. I remember now that family and friends constantly told me when I was young that I worried too much. "Hijito, don't worry so much." "J-M, stop worrying." "Son, why do you worry so much?" Did I have anxiety and panic attacks as a child? Did I repress them for decades? Self-medicated solutions worked for so many years after I found alcohol at age fourteen. Binge drinking began at eighteen. Maybe anxiety is triggered by a past event that escapes into our future. I try to stop thinking about my past, about tomorrow. But I am so nostalgic for tomorrow.*

JUNE 9, 2012 – *I tell my family at dinner I want to be cremated when I die.*

JUNE 15, 2012 – "Obama Suspends Deportation for Thousands of Illegals, Tells GOP Pass DREAM Act." *Fox News*

JUNE 27, 2012 – "Arizona's 'Show-Me-Your-Papers' Law Rolls Out a Day After Supreme Court Ruling." *CNN*

JULY 2, 2012 – "In the First Quarter of 2012, 865 Bills and Resolutions Relating to Immigrants and Refugees Were Introduced in 45 State Legislatures and the District of Columbia." *Congressional Record*

JULY 2, 2012 – *I wake up hoping I won't be anxious on my birthday. My forty-second birthday. I act happy all day, trying not to worry about how many birthdays I will see in my lifetime. My eleven-year-old daughter asks me, "Dad, do you remember when you turned twelve?" "I can't think about my past anymore." She looks at me with both sadness and bewilderment and laughs anxiously. "Dad, you worry too much."*

JULY 3, 2012 – *Heart palpitations, PVCs, begin for the first time in my life; they will haunt me for the rest of it. I lie in bed all day, worried about raising my* *heart rate too high. Worried they will return in a minute, an hour, a day, a week. I lie motionless in bed, my finger frozen on my neck taking my pulse. 1, 2, 3, 4, 5, 6, 7, 8, 9, 10. I match my heart rate to my watch. I press my neck so often in 2012 that a rash forms where my carotid artery is buried under my skin. My neck smells of hydrocortisone for the remainder of the year.*

JULY 8, 2012 –

JULY 12, 2012 – "In the Age of Anxiety, Are We All Mentally Ill?" *Reuters*

AUGUST 1, 2012 – "Mild Mental Illness 'Raises Risk of Premature Death.'" *BBC News*

AUGUST 5, 2012 – *I think of suicide. But I am too scared to die. I worry that I will come back as an unmoored ghost, still anxious and untethered to any family, any history, any people, any reality, just energy floating without purpose. I am resolved to remain a half-life, a being too anxious to fully live. Am I a specter now?*

AUGUST 8, 2012 – "Be Careful When Diagnosing Your Ailments Online." *CNN Business*

AUGUST 12, 2012 – "For Most Undocumented Immigrants, Life in the Shadows Continues." *Washington Post*

AUGUST 23, 2012 – "Fingerprint Records Reveal 825,000 Immigrants with Multiple Names, Inconsistent Birth Dates." *NextGov*

AUGUST 25, 2012 – *Pulse under control. No PVCs for weeks. No panic attacks for weeks. I am worried they will soon return.*

SEPTEMBER 2, 2012 – "Heavy Drinking Rewires Brain, Increasing Susceptibility to Anxiety Problems." *Science Daily*

SEPTEMBER 15, 2012 – *I am still OK.*

OCTOBER 31, 2012 – "World Digital Library Adds *Florentine Codex.*" *Library of Congress*

NOVEMBER 8, 2012 – "Los Angeles City Council Approves ID & Debit Cards for Undocumented Immigrants." *KPCC*

NOVEMBER 10, 2012 – *Anxiety descends into a deep depression. I call my mom crying. Please help. I am ashamed to let my daughter know that I am sad, that I am out of control. The images in my mind won't stop. I am too ashamed to tell my wife and let my daughter know that Daddy is suffering a mental crisis. I am too ashamed to go to the doctor. I'm too ashamed to get any help.*

NOVEMBER 11, 2012 – *My wife is frustrated by my anxiety but compassionate. Healthy people really don't understand mental illness. Before 2012, I was the same way. If you can't see the pain on the afflicted body, does it exist? I can see she is sad, worried, scared for me. Scared for herself. I worry she will leave me for a healthy person. Between my anger and my exhaustion, she talks me into going to the doctor and getting help. She has to drive me. I am too panicked to drive. I am too afraid I will find myself under the cement bridge that began this whole spiral. I feel so exhausted when I enter the room. The doctor enters the room. I have never met her before. The door shuts. We talk for two hours . . . In the end, she puts me on Lexapro and gives me Xanax for when I have panic attacks. I worry it will not work.*

NOVEMBER 12, 2012 – *I take my first Lexapro. I feel a euphoria that scares more than relieves me. I call the doctor, the pharmacist, panicking. The pharmacist calls back first. I feel like a wave of heat has entered my brain and is going through my body, I tell him. I feel like I am going to die. You are not going to die, he says. The medicine is regulating your lack of serotonin. It will help. Give it a few days, and if you are dizzy go see your doctor. Cut the pill in* *half and start slow, but call your doctor. I read the side effects all day. Pacing through the house searching for the effects with every step.*

NOVEMBER 29, 2012 – "NASA Warns Mayan Apocalypse Stories Pose Threat to Frightened Children and Teenagers." *Daily Mail*

DECEMBER 1, 2012 – "For Better or Worse, 90 Percent of World's Data Generated in Last Two Years." *Science Daily*

DECEMBER 8, 2012 – "Why Are We All So Anxious?" *Daily Mail*

DECEMBER 19, 2012 – "Chatter of Doomsday Makes Beijing Nervous." *New York Times*

DECEMBER 19, 2012 – "Michigan Secretary of State Sued for Denying Driver's Licenses to Undocumented Immigrants." *NPR*

DECEMBER 20, 2012 – "Mayan Apocalypse: China Arrests Nearly 1,000 Doomsday 'Cult' Members." *The Telegraph*

DECEMBER 20, 2012 – "Final Countdown: 1 Day Until the Mayan Apocalypse." *Liberty Voice*

DECEMBER 21, 2012 – "After Mayan Apocalypse Failure, Believers May Suffer." *Live Science*

DECEMBER 22, 2012 – "Mayan Apocalypse: FB Group's Mass Suicide in Argentina Averted." *Guardian*

DECEMBER 24, 2012 – "Obama Administration Deported Record 1.5 Million People." *NPR*

DECEMBER 25, 2012 – *I don't think of my death as much anymore, and I am not nearly as anxious. I still worry. Lexapro staves off the ghosts most of the day. It seems to have the effect of making me unable to see any ghosts, any haunting images from the past or in my unknowable future. I can't find any documentation on this side effect. I keep searching.*

DECEMBER 27, 2012 –

DECEMBER 31, 2012 – *Resolution: Don't worry about tomorrow. Get off Lexapro. I miss the ghosts.*

✳

JULY 8, 2019 – *My daughter tells me that the apocalypse did happen in 2012 and that the world did end. We are living in a black hole and this is an alternate universe. We are all ghosts now. There is even a test to show you. Take it. Really, Dad, there is a Twitter feed that has documented it for years. She smiles and walks away.*

JULY 8, 2020 – *Anxiety is there. It is only sleeping. Its breath quivers perpetually through man's being.*

BOOK V
Omens

Dark night

wanting to investigate

We seek secret things

paths forbidden

cries of the living

We search for apparitions in the fragrance of things,

in

auguries

placed here.

(HANGING) TREES

Lynchings & mob violence to enforce white supremacy:
highlighting victims of Mexican Origin, 1849-1928

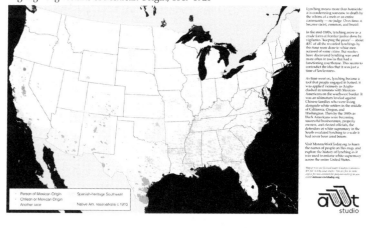

*

There is an unknown document to be named that reveals that 2,356 trees and 4,500 feet of rope were used to lynch Mexicans. Here lie the names of known and unknown Mexicans who were lynched.

Unknown Mexican, CA, 1849. Unknown Mexican, CA, 1849. Juan Chapa Guerra, CA, 1850. Francisco Flores, TX, 1850. Pablo [?], CA, 1851. Antonio Cruz and Patricio Janori, CA, 1851. Josefa Segovia, CA, 1851. Domingo [?], CA, 1851. Two unknown Mexicans, CA, 1851. Patricio Chaves and Domingo Ramón Apodaca, 1852. Carlos Esclava, CA, 1852. [?] Flores, CA, 1852. Unknown Mexican, TX, 1852. Unknown Mexican, TX, 1852. Six unknown Mexicans, TX, 1852. Two unknown Mexicans, CA, 1852. John Balthus, CA, 1852. José Cheverino, CA, 1852. Cruz Flores, CA, 1852. Domingo Hernández, CA, 1852. Capistrano López and unknown Mexican, CA, 1852. [?] Pansa, CA, 1852. Doroteo Zavaleta and Jesús Rivas, CA, 1852. Reyes Feliz, CA, 1852. Cipriano Sandoval, Benito López, and [?] Barumas, CA, 1852. Gabriel Luhan and José de la Cruz Vigil, NM, 1852. Big Bill, CA, 1853. Unknown Mexican, CA, 1853. Unknown Mexican, CA, 1853. Two unknown Mexicans, CA, 1853. Antonio Valencia, CA, 1853. Juan Sánchez, CA, 1853. Polonio Sánchez, CA, 1853. José María Ochoa, CA, 1853. Bernardo Daniel, [?] Higuerro, and three unknown Mexicans, CA, 1853. Dolores [?] and unknown Mexican, CA, 1854. Nemesio Berreyesa, CA, 1854. Unknown Mexican, CA, 1854. José Higuera, CA, 1854. Mateo Andrade, CA, 1854. Salvador Valdez, CA, 1855. Four unknown Mexicans, NM, 1855. Justo Betancour, TX, 1855. Four unknown Mexicans, TX, 1855. [?] Trancolino, [?] Puertovino, and José [?], CA, 1855. Manuel Castro, CA, 1855. Rafael Escobar, CA, 1855. Unknown Mexican, CA, 1855. Manuel García and at least six unknown Mexicans, CA, 1855. Francisco Tapia, Jesús Pino, and Francisco Sánchez, CA, 1855. Unknown Mexican, TX, 1855. Unknown Mexican, CA, 1855. Three unknown Mexicans, CA, 1856. Unknown Mexican, TX, 1856. José Castro, CA, 1856. Diego Navarro, Pedro López, Juan Valenzuela, Miguel Soto, Juan Catabo, and two unknown Mexicans, CA, 1857. José Jesús Espinosa, CA, 1857. Encarnación Berreyesa, CA, 1857. Francisco or Guerro Ardillero, CA, 1857. Three unknown Mexicans, CA, 1857. Juan Flores, CA, 1857. José Anastacio García, CA, 1857. Mexican Joe, CA, 1857. José Santos, CA, 1857. Manuel Ribera, NM, 1857. Eight unknown Mexicans, TX, 1857.

Unknown Mexican, TX, 1857. Unknown Mexican, TX, 1857. Jesús Anastasia, TX, 1858. Carlos Martínez, NM, 1858. Unknown Mexican, NM, 1858. Santos Peralta, CA, 1858. Nicano Urdiales, Pablo Longoria, Francisco Huizano, and Felipe López, TX, 1858. Joaquín Valenzuela and Luciano Tapia, CA, 1858. Pío Linares, CA, 1858. Miguel Blanco, Rafael Herreda, and Desiderio Grijalva, CA, 1858. José Antonio García, CA, 1858. Nieves Robles, CA, 1858. Pancho Daniel, CA, 1858. Four unknown Mexicans, CA, 1858. Rafael Polaco, AZ, 1859. Francisco Badillo and son, CA, 1859. Tomás Cabrera, TX, 1859. Unknown Mexican, AZ, 1859. Unknown Mexican, CO, 1860. Mateo García, AZ, 1860. Unknown Mexican, AZ, 1860. Unknown Mexican, NM, 1861. Unknown Mexican, AZ, 1861. José Claudio Alvitre, CA, 1861. F. Ramírez, CA, 1861. Francisco Cota, CA, 1861. Tom "The Spaniard," CA, 1861. José Olivas and José Yreba, CA, 1863. Unknown Mexican, CA, 1863. Manuel Cerredel, CA, 1863. Luis Seyra and Cosme Núñez, CA, 1863. Joe Pizanthia (aka Spaniard Frank), MO, 1864. Patricinio López, CA, 1864. Jesús Arellanes, CA, 1864. José Aniceto, [?] Balbenbro, and Simón Montoya, NV, 1864. Unknown Mexican, CA, 1864. Unknown Mexican, CA, 1864. Juan Higuera, CA, 1865. Unknown Mexican, CO, 1866. Juan Valenzuela, CA, 1866. Unknown Mexican, CA, 1877. Seven unknown Mexicans, TX, 1868. S. Robles, CA, 1869. Unknown Mexican, NM, 1869. José Ortega and Luciano García, NV, 1870. Valentine Varaga, Jesús Gómez, and Gregorio Gómez, CA, 1870. Juan de Dios Sepúlveda, CA, 1870. Sacramento Duarte, CA, 1870. Unknown Mexican, CO, 1870. Miguel Lachenal, CA, 1870. Donacino Sánchez, CO, 1871. Pablo García (aka Quemado) and Tomás the Chihuahuanian, NM, 1870. Diego Lucero, NM, 1871. Unknown Mexican, CO, 1871. Pablo Padilla, NM, 1871. Juan Sandobal, NM, 1872. Unknown Mexican, TX, 1872. Juan Castro, CA, 1872. José Segura, NM, 1872. Unknown Mexican, TX, 1872. Merijilodo Martinis, CO, 1873. Domingo García, AZ, 1872. Mariano Tisnado, AZ, 1873. Nine unknown Mexicans, AZ, 1873. Two unknown Mexicans, AZ, 1873. Leonardo Córdoba Clemente López and Jesús Saguaripa, AZ, 1873. Two unknown Mexicans, CO, 1873. Unknown female

Mexican, CO, 1873. Three unknown Mexicans, CO, 1873. Lucas Lugas, AZ, 1873. Manuel Subiate, AZ, 1873. Unknown Mexican, TX, 1873. Filomeno Ríos, Jorge Rodríguez, José M. Reinas, Epifanio Ríos, Blas Mata, Vicente García, and Leonardo Garza, TX, 1873. Pedro Patrón, Isidoro Padilla, Dario Juan Balagan, and José Candelaria, NM, 1873. Severanio Apodaca and four unknown Mexicans, NM, 1873. Indian Charley, CO, 1874. Tomás Valencia, NM, 1874. Juan Correro García, NM, 1874. Jesús Romo (aka El Gordo), CA, 1874. Juan and his two sons Antonio and Marcelo, TX, 1874. Three unknown Mexicans, TX, 1874. Mateo Robles, TX, 1874. Gabriel Leyva, TX, 1874. Lupe Vaca and Isidoro Anaya, AZ, 1874. Francisco Ramírez, TX, 1874. Unknown Mexican, NM, 1874. Antonio Guerra and Pedro Garza, TX, 1874. Ventura Núñez, AZ, 1874. Unknown Mexican, TX, 1874. Unknown Mexican, TX, 1874. Two unknown Mexicans, TX, 1875. Two unknown Mexicans, TX, 1875. Jesús Mes, Pat Mes, Thomas Madrid, and Jermin Aguirre, NM, 1875. Cruz Vega, NM, 1875. Manuel Cardinas, NM, 1875. R. García and J. Elvira, CA, 1875. José Ygarra, CA, 1875. Antone [?], CA, 1875. Pancho Cruz and Ramón Mes, NM, 1875. Anastacio Pérez, Ponciano Lerma, and Emilio González, TX, 1876. Eight unknown Mexicans, TX, 1876. Three unknown Mexicans, TX, 1876. Juan Trujillo, CO, 1876. José María Miera, NM, 1876. Melitón Córdoba, Gregorio Miera, and Juan Miera, NM, 1876. Juan Buenvidas and Crespin Gallegos, NM, 1876. Nica Meras, NM, 1876. Jesús Largo, NM, 1876. José Chamales and Francisco Arias, CA, 1877. Five unknown Mexicans, TX, 1877. Two unknown Mexicans, TX, 1877. Justin Arajo, CA, 1877. Marcos González, CO, 1877. Andrés Barela, NM, 1877. Antonio Maron, Francisco Encinas, Miguel Elías, Ferman Eideo, and Bessena Ruiz, CA, 1877. Unknown Mexicans, CO, 1878. Refugio Montallo Baca, CA, 1878. Unknown Mexican, TX, 1878. Manuel Barela, NM, 1879. Romolo or Ramino Baca, NM, 1879. Francisco Sandoval, NM, 1879. Juan Graviel, CO, 1880. Paz Chávez, NM, 1880. Juanito Mes, NM, 1880. Refugio Ramírez, his wife, Silvester García Ramírez, and his daughter María Inés Ramírez, TX, 1880. José María Salazar, AZ, 1880. Antonius Mestes, CO, 1880. Pantaleón Mieran and Santos Benavidas, NM, 1880. Matías Alcantar, NV, 1881. California Joe, Escolástico Perea, and Miguel Berrera, NM, 1881. Unknown Mexican, TX, 1881. Faustino Gutiérrez, NM, 1881. Two unknown Mexicans, NM, 1881. José Ordona, AZ, 1881. Onofre Baca, NM, 1881. Narciso Montoya, NM, 1881. Miguel Tarazona, Joaquín Montano, José Samaniego, and Reinaldo Samaniego, AZ, 1881. Nine unknown Mexicans, AZ, 1881. Waken [?], NM, 1881. Selzo Espinosa, Aristotle Noranjo, and Fernando Chávez, NM, 1881. Francisco Tafoya, NM, 1882. Pedro Gómez and Pablo Aguilar, NM, 1882. Juan Alvarid (Elervad), NM, 1882. Guadalupe Archuleta, NM, 1882. Two unknown Mexicans, TX, 1883. Pedro Quintinilla, TX, 1883. Unknown Mexican, TX, 1883. Encarnación García, CA, 1883. Unknown Mexican, CO, 1883. Unknown Mexican, CO, 1883. Four unknown Mexicans, TX, 1884. [?] Chaves, NM, 1884. Juan Castillo, CO, 1884. Luciano Padilla, NE, 1884. José Trujello Gallegos, NM, 1885. Vicente Olivas, CA, 1886. Andrés Martínez and José María Cadena, TX, 1886. Pedro Peña and Mateo Cadena, TX, 1886. Gus Kernwood, WY, 1886. Three unknown Mexicans, TX, 1887. Cecilio Ybarra and Viviano Díaz, TX, 1887. José María Casas and Gerardo Contreras, TX, 1887. Mat Pettis and Reto, TX, 1888. Santos Salazar, TX, 1888. Two unknown Mexicans, NM, 1889. Unknown Mexican, NM, 1890. Unknown Mexican, TX, 1890. Jesús Salceda, TX, 1891. Francisco Torres, CA, 1892. Patricio Maes, NM, 1892. Ireneo González, NM, 1893. Jesús Fuen, CA, 1893. Antonio Martínez, Antonio José García, and Victoriano Aragón, NM, 1893. Celio Lucero, NV, 1893. Charlie Williams, LA, 1894. Luis Moreno, CA, 1895. Florentine Suaste, TX, 1895. James Umbra and Mexican John, OK, 1895. Aureliano Castellán, TX, 1896. Unknown Mexican, TX, 1897. Marcelo Tijeras, AZ, 1897. Carlos Guillén, TX, 1898. Ignacio Rivera, AZ, 1901. Felix Martínez, TX, 1901. Carlos Muñoz, TX, 1905. Michael Rodríguez, TX, 1910. Unknown Mexican, TX, 1911. Antonio Gómez, TX, 1911. Adolfo Padilla, NM, 1914. Alejos Arguijo, TX, 1914. Juan González, NE, 1915. Hilario [?], José [?], and María León, AZ, 1915. Lorenzo and Gorgonio Manríquez, TX, 1915. Rudolfo Muñoz, TX, 1915. Desiderio Flores, Antonio Flores, and

Desiderio Flores Jr., TX, 1915. Eusebio Hernández, TX, 1915. Abraham Salinas and Juan Tobar, TX, 1915. Francisco Becanegra and unknown Mexican, TX, 1915. Three unknown Mexicans, TX, 1915. Two unknown Mexicans, TX, 1915. Six unknown Mexicans, TX, 1915. Fourteen unknown Mexicans, TX, 1915. Three unknown Mexicans, TX, 1915. Three unknown Mexicans, TX, 1915. Ygnacio Rincones, Alejos Vela, and Angel Rivera, TX, 1915. Unknown Mexican, TX, 1915. Unknown Mexican, TX, 1915. Unknown Mexican, TX, 1915. Unknown Mexican, TX, 1915. Unknown Mexican, TX, 1915. Unknown Mexican, TX, 1915. Unknown Mexican, TX, 1915. Unknown Mexican, TX, 1915. Unknown Mexican, TX, 1915. Unknown Mexican, TX, 1915. Refugio Pérez, TX, 1915. Alberto Cantú, TX, 1915. Juan Nepemuceno Rodríguez, TX, 1915. [?] Ebenoza, TX, 1915. Jesús Bazan and [?] Longorio, TX, 1915. Juan Niete, TX, 1915. Trinidad Ybarra, Manuel Severe, Santiago Salas, and six unknown Mexicans, TX, 1915. Manuel Robles, TX, 1915. Juan Tevar, TX, 1915. Victoriano Ponce and José Morin, TX, 1916. Gerónimo Lerma, TX, 1916. Pedro [?], Bivanio [?], Sibranio [?], [?] Flores, Ramón [?], Tiburcio [?], Alberto [?], Macadonio [?], [?] Huerte, Eutemio [?], [?] González, Manuel [?], Antonio [?], Pedro[?], TX, 1918. Florencio García, TX, 1918. José González and Santos Ortez, TX, 1918. Elías Villareal Zarate, TX, 1922. Tomás Núñez and his two sons, TX, 1926. Rafael Benevidas, NM, 1928. Unknown Mexican.

Unknown   Mexican.   Unknown   Mexican.   Unknown   Mexican.
Unknown   Mexican.   Unknown   Mexican.   Unknown   Mexican.
Unknown   Mexican.   Unknown   Mexican.   Unknown   Mexican.
Unknown   Mexican.   Unknown   Mexican.   Unknown   Mexican.
Unknown   Mexican.   Unknown   Mexican.   Unknown   Mexican.
Unknown   Mexican.   Unknown   Mexican.   Unknown   Mexican.
Unknown   Mexican.   Unknown   Mexican.   Unknown   Mexican.
Unknown   Mexican.   Unknown   Mexican.   Unknown   Mexican.
Unknown   Mexican.   Unknown   Mexican.   Unknown   Mexican.
Unknown   Mexican.   Unknown   Mexican.   Unknown   Mexican.
Unknown   Mexican.   Unknown   Mexican.   Unknown   Mexican.
Unknown   Mexican.   Unknown   Mexican.   Unknown   Mexican.
Unknown   Mexican.   Unknown   Mexican.   Unknown   Mexican.
Unknown Mexican. Unknown Mexican . . .

*

Everyone knows how disdainfully the Mexican race is treated in general; everyone knows that Mexicans are treated worse than Negroes. Mexicans cannot enter hotels, restaurants, and other public places there. The doors of public schools are closed to the children of our race, semi-savage Americans use Mexicans for target practice. How many men of our race have died because a blond savage has gotten a notion to test his skill with weapons by firing at them, without there even being any dispute between them! In the so-called court of law, Mexicans are judged, generally with no formalities at all, and are sentenced to be hanged or to suffer harsh punishment, without there being any proof or even the slightest hint that they might have committed the crime for which they are punished.

-RICARDO FLORES MAGÓN,
"THE REPERCUSSIONS OF A LYNCHING," 1910-

Hanging trees are rooted deep within the historical landscape of the
United States; some still stand while others are cut down to allow
America to bury its lynching past. The ghost of a hanging tree found
me in the spring of 2018 when I went to Pueblo, Colorado, to visit El
Pueblo History Museum and see the Treaty of Guadalupe Hidalgo.
This was the first time the treaty, which had profound effects on
Pueblo, found itself in Colorado. When it was signed in 1848, parts of
the city's south side, with the stroke of a pen, were assigned a new
identity; they now "belonged" to the United States. Usually buried
within the documents of the National Archives in D.C., the treaty
was the first formative document to define the rights and status of

Mexicans in the United States. I traveled three hours from Denver to Pueblo to see it, expecting to be awestruck. I stared at it for as long as I could, seeing if I could uncover its lived history or be moved by the weight of its effects on Mexicans for generations. This was the document that would annex thousands of miles of Mexican land to the United States, in the process creating the border that today still defines who is documented and who is undocumented. This is the document that made me and millions of others hyphenated undocumented subjects of a nation-state. I kept telling myself this over and over. Nothing. The weight of its paper and ink had no effect. My eyes instead were drawn to a piece of wood held in the museum like a rare document, the Hanging Tree of El Pueblo.

Held within feet of the temporary Treaty of Guadalupe Hidalgo exhibit was an elaborate permanent exhibit of the cross section of Old Monarch, a tree that was a purported "hanging tree," though no one knows for sure who was hanged on it during the hundreds of years it stood in what is now the main street of Pueblo. Vague newspaper records indicate that fourteen men were hanged there between the treaty's signing in 1848 and the 1880s, though no one knows who or exactly when. The full archive is erased but the act of hanging in full display in the mind's eye. I am taken by the weight of its presence. The Treaty of Guadalupe Hidalgo kept this hanging tree half-dead, half-alive; it was a perpetual specter haunting all those who came to see the treaty, reminding me that its limbs were as divisive as the ink and parchment of the treaty. I stare and wonder whether this cross section was used to brace the nooses around Mexican necks. It isn't impossible to believe, after all, since Pueblo hanged José González as late as 1919. No one knows which tree they used for that hanging. I am told that I can visit a plaque where the Hanging Tree once stood in downtown Pueblo. I drive to the location of the tree and find the plaque:

SITE OF SOUTH PUEBLO'S HANGING TREE

June 25, 1883 – 338 rings – first growth 1545.

"Old Monarch," cut down in South Pueblo on June 25, 1883, was 388 years old, had a circumference of 29 feet and was 88 feet tall. It proudly served as the oldest tree landmark in what later became the State of Colorado and stood as a testament to the fertility of the Arkansas River Valley soil.

Stories tell of 14 men that were hanged from one of its limbs at different times. The first white woman that died in Colorado is said to have been buried under its sprawling branches.

Though recorded history cannot validate these colorful claims, the magnificent Cottonwood eventually became known as the "Hanging Tree." The day came, however, when the value of the tree in the middle of the main business street was challenged. In spite of 366 protesting citizens, the South Pueblo Council ordered it to be cut down. Men hired by the Council approached the tree and informed the gathering crowd that they were only there to trim the branches. This, of course, was the news the protesters wanted to hear and soon dispersed. As soon as the crowd had gone, the Council sent orders to girdle the tree. Once that task was done all hope of saving "Old Monarch" was lost.

What is erased from the plaque is what happens to the highly visible body when you are hanged in public. If the rope is long enough and the noose tied correctly, you die near instantaneously. Your cervical spinal cord will be severed and this "spinal shock" instantly kills you, as your blood pressure and consciousness drop to zero in milliseconds. All too often, however, the rope was too short and the branches too weak, and the victim thrashed around for up to five minutes, struggling and suffocating on their own blood, gasping for air while their brain slowly "coned"— the physiological process where your spine and brain are compressed and your brain hemorrhages. In such a case, your heart continues to beat for up to twenty or thirty minutes after you are hanged. How much awareness a victim possesses or the amount of pain suffered is unknown.

Near the plaque is an old café now called the Hanging Tree Café, where they sell memento mori shirts and mugs with pictures of skulls and crossbones. I suspect the owner felt a noose image would be in poor taste. I enter and sit down, look at the menu—they only serve Mexican food. On the wall is an advertisement for a Pueblo ghost tour to kick off the Halloween season; the highlighted attraction: the Hanging Tree of El Pueblo. I wonder if the Treaty of Guadalupe Hidalgo will still be on display.

AMEXICA

A specter is haunting the United States—the specter of Amexica. All the powers of old America have entered into a holy alliance to exorcise this specter: Trump, Sessions, and Miller; J. P. Morgan and Chase and Fox News; the alt-right and ICE.

Karl Marx was only partially correct. Racial specters live forever.

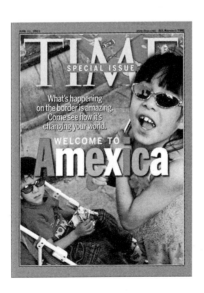

The border is vanishing before our eyes, creating a New World for all of us.

In 2001, the year I began my work as a Latinx scholar at the University of Colorado at Boulder, *Time* magazine declared that the browning of America was upon us. On the front cover of the magazine, a photojournalist captures two young Mexican children staring at the public through sunglasses. The children become haunting images for white America, representing the new demographics of the United States, substantiating the fact that more immigrant children are being born in the United States than white children, a fact that Fox News commentators decry to foment fear among their viewership. And as white America gazes on their brown bodies at newsstands, in supermarket lines, and in its homes, it wonders how to include these people in its life. White Americans already see them at every service counter in their neighborhood, in the kitchens, and on their lawns. Those who are truly "woke" will let Latinxs serve as nannies, and, god forbid, one may even enter the gene pool through a cousin they see only on Thanksgiving.

In 2001, Bush Jr. understood what Amexica meant for big business, as he would declare in a joint press conference with President Vicente Fox: "[Mexicans] are willing to do the jobs others in America aren't willing to do. We ought to welcome that person to the country and we ought to make that a legal part of our economy." For Bush it came down to dollars and cents. Immigrants can pay for their documents by becoming laborers. Covered on every news channel, newspaper, and talk show, Bush's appeal to the public was that Mexicans should do the work that Americans would not: they would groom American lawns, raise their children, clean their homes, pick their produce, and even, in the case of the Bushes, marry into the family and produce Latinx children who can run for office as Republicans and groom a new conservative constituent. In 2001, for Bush, the answer was not to build a wall paid for by Mexico; his answer was built on a capitalist platform of "compassionate conservatism" and the documentation of immigrants as laboring workers within the capitalist system. Welcome to Amexica. Here is your rake.

*

Hispanics: 1970 to 2050

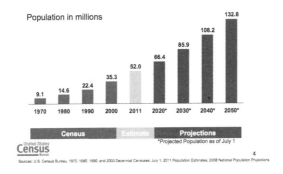

Population in millions

1970	1980	1990	2000	2011	2020*	2030*	2040*	2050*
9.1	14.6	22.4	35.3	52.0	66.4	85.9	108.2	132.8

Census	Estimate	Projections

*Projected Population as of July 1

Census
United States Census Bureau

4

Sources: U.S. Census Bureau, 1970, 1980, 1990, and 2000 Decennial Censuses; July 1, 2011 Population Estimates; 2008 National Population Projections

The same year that *Time* magazine announces this changing demographic, I find myself giving a talk at the Boulder International Film Festival, introducing Guillermo Gómez-Peña's *The Great Mojado Invasion, Part 2.* I am contacted by the organizer of the festival. I do not work on film, nor have I seen the movie, but I am the only Mexican for miles, and I suspect they feel that they need a Mexican to introduce the film. I watch the film and see that it engages with the xenophobic rhetoric that is permeating the airwaves and newsstands at the time the browning of America is being studied. It is a counter to Pat Buchanan's 2001 *New York Times* best-selling book *The Death of the West: How Dying Populations and Immigrant Invasions Imperil Our Country and Civilization*, which argues that the West is dying, the United States is dying, our civilization is dying, all because of the "plague" perpetuated by migrant Mexican bodies. To Buchanan and others on Fox News, immigration is not a cause for celebration of a new Amexica, but rather the cause of the death of the status quo, a violent end to the glorious white city on the hill. To Buchanan, America has become a ghost town run by Mexican zombies who, through Reconquista—the alt-right conspiratorial notion that Mexicans are taking back the United States—will erase all that white America has done to create a great Christian nation. Gómez-Peña's work is a counter to this hundred-year-old narrative. A mockumentary, *The Great Mojado Invasion* samples hundreds of yards of found footage depicting Mexican stereotypes perpetuated in Hollywood for generations. It shows Mexicans having taken over the United States and established a new "Mexican regime," under which Anglos have become second-class citizens and work as laborers in the new economy. White America has died, its citizens having become Marx's laboring specters, and Mexicans have been resurrected as its bourgeois leaders, its saviors.

Gómez-Peña does not make the trip to Boulder, so I am left alone onstage to represent the film. After the film, I begin the talk to an all-white audience with the headline from *Time* magazine and a line from the film: "Welcome to Amexica! Show me your papers." The joke falls flat. No one laughs. I quickly become the young child on the *Time* cover. They stare, size me up, wonder who I am. Like the young children, onstage, I become one of the thousands of images in the film. I am not a professor. They see right through me. I am a specter of Amexica. I want to put on sunglasses and stare back but am left stuttering with a lisp. I revert to being that boy I once was on the bus in the middle of the playground in L.A., talking into the microphone . . . A, B, C . . .

INTERLUDE

AN INQUIRY INTO THE "MEXICAN QUESTION"

What is the ... ?

What are they called and why?

What does a good one look like?

What does a bad one look like?

What is the origin of these people?

What place do they inhabit, and what are their characteristics?

What are the names given to this group, and what is their etymological origin?

What is their degree of culture?

What were their cultural contributions?

What are their moral virtues?

What are their defects?

What is their physical appearance?

What language do they speak?

-QUESTIONNAIRE USED TO CREATE THE *FLORENTINE CODEX*, 1566-

*

Of all strange corners of our strange West, this is the strangest; and it is a chosen and beloved abiding place of the strangest and least comprehensible of all those who make up our national character.

... In the burning noontide comes a slow gray burro, meek and patient; his head drooped, his eyes mere glinting peepholes in his outward shagginess,—every line, curve, and movement full of unobtrusive dignity. And this sedate aspect eminently befits his estate, for he is no ordinary beast; he is bearer of the presiding genius of the desert—the mestizo, the Greaser, half-blood offspring of the marriage of antiquity and modernity. Time cannot take from him the unmistakable impress of old Spain. But his Spanish appearance is not his dominant characteristic. His skin has been sunbrowned for centuries; his nose and cheeks are broad; his lips are thick;

his brows are heavy, his sheltering eyes soft, passionate, inscrutable. King in his own natural right, master of a blessed content, he is the strange progeny of parents who waged warfare against each other, and all but perished in the strife.... Anomalous as he is, he is one of the few distinct types in our national life whose origin is fully known to us....

As all this goes to make manly character, the Greaser, a mere fragment of a man in stature [sic]. According to the artistic dictum, which pronounces the curve and the line of beauty, the Greaser should assuredly be beautiful, for his make-up is superlatively rich in curves. His pudgy head and face bear an obtrusive lot of curling lines, which wriggle sinuously down the neck and shoulders, until they are lost in the portentous curve of his waistband. For he is fat. Rich or poor, idler or loafer, he never runs to leanness. The women are like the men. Perhaps you have heard or read of beautiful mestizo maidens? Traveler's tales! Save in the pictures of susceptible romanticists, I have never seen a beautiful Greaser girl.

-WILLIAM LIGHTON, "THE GREASER," 1899-

At what moment in U.S. history did questions about Mexican documentality enter the national imaginary? If the *Florentine Codex* is the work that defines the early modern foundations of Mexican documentality, which the questionnaire above illustrates, then the emergence of the Mexican Question in the mid-nineteenth century becomes the modern moment when the Mexican emerges as *the* "documented subject," and this marks the beginnings of Mexicans as specters of the state's bureaucratic information systems. This question finds its roots in the nineteenth century, and specifically around the U.S.-Mexico War of 1846–48 and the Treaty of Guadalupe Hidalgo of 1847–48. Here at this midpoint I want to spend a little time setting the historical foundations of documentality and its relationship to the Mexican Question because it is so central to how Mexicans, and, arguably, to some degree, all Latinxs, are documented or undocumented, so please indulge my historical digressions.

At its core the Mexican Question is interested in defining the "rights and status of Mexicans," which, in effect, is an inquiry into how the state documents the Mexican. The desire to document is a colonial endeavor founded on a need to have not only the power to inscribe Mexicans within an emerging paper world but also the capacity to erase Mexicans with the same pen that inscribed them. To this end, this question about the rights and status of the Other is a desire to have the authority to document, both to give life and control through paper and, with the same pen, to erase the object of the inquiry. The Mexican Question, then, is a sine qua non for making the Mexican into a spectral object of the state, a political subject who is written into life and death through a rhetorical inquest into their Otherness. At the same time, ironically, the Mexican Question haunts an expanding United States with every document created, with every inscription published and catalogued.

The Mexican Question was a European-American inquiry into the documentation of Mexicans that found its rhetorical dimensions within the parameters of democratic expansion and the embodied racialization of the Mexican peoples who lived in "terra incognita." The discursive origins of the Mexican Question found their place of dissemination in documents in American print culture, and the epigraph that opens this interlude begins to reveal the racial constellations that the question mapped. Published in the prestigious *Atlantic*, William Lighton's "The Greaser" attests to the centrality of the founding Enlightenment questions concerning democratic statecraft, documentality, race, geography, and Mexican spectrality itself in the nineteenth-century United States' emerging document culture. According to Lighton, it was in the "strangest" of "all strange corners of our strange West" that Americans would raise the question of the "natural rights" of the Greaser, who is "a mere fragment of a man in stature." We begin to see that raising the question of the natural rights of Mexicans and the rights that Anglos have to their lands foreshadowed the contradictions that otherness and terra incognita would present to America's enlightened inquest into transcontinental dominance. This contradiction is where the specter emerges, for it haunts the ideological apparatus that defines a people's colonial reality. Inquiry into the Other is a metaphysical inquiry into the spectral, the "thing" that cannot be defined with the known documented language that has enabled colonial dominance.

Echoing Rousseau and Hobbes, Lighton's "The Greaser" locates the "mestizo" Mexican within the strange frontier territory in order to posit him as the prepolitical "savage man," the spectral antithesis of the civilized political subject known as the Christian American man. Lighton's Greaser stands as the haunted figure of political subjectivity who has rights precisely, as Lighton suggests, because he is an amalgamation of both the European Spanish and Indian races, a mestizo. The Greaser is simultaneously the "king in his own natural right"—and thus bestowed with certain rights, freedoms, powers, and obligations—and a mestizo, whose racial character and geographic ignorance locates him as a semicivilized political object, a savage man without "reason." This allows Lighton to posit his Greaser as Rousseau's savage, a prepolitical person who inhabits the undefined terra incognita against which the American Enlightened imagination of the East would define civilization. This, in turn, allows the American citizenry to reaffirm its ontological status as *the natural* political people of U.S. democratic culture and Mexicans as the othered *ethnos*, the specter of terra incognita. As a specter of the state, Mexican "Greasers" would never be given the authority to document their own rights and status but rather would remain the object of colonial documentation.

Lighton's "The Greaser," along with the hundreds of similar essays about the rights and status of Mexicans in the United States, may have found its discursive impetus in the strangeness of the frontier, but the explosion of American print culture facilitated the circulation of stories of Mexican peoplehood related to the Mexican Question, beginning in U.S. literary magazines in the 1840s, the years when Manifest Destiny took hold of American democracy and, not coincidentally, mass cultural forms emerged. It is important to remember that magazines were the first and only medium of widespread public communication and the main form of mass documentation at that time. During the period of territorial expansion, there were no radio or film industries, no official national newspapers, and no other regular medium of information and entertainment that reached a national audience except for magazines. The "house magazines," such as *Scribner's*, *The Century*, *Harper's*, and *The Atlantic*, which were the preferred literary and cultural magazines of the middle class on the East Coast, sold over 250,000 copies each.

William Lighton's "The Greaser" was merely following a long line of inquiries into the Mexican that found their origins fifty-five years prior. In the spring of 1845, John O'Sullivan, editor and founder of the *Democratic Review*, sat down to write two essays that would reveal much about the territorial and racial dimensions of democracy: "Annexation" and "The Mexican Question." In "Annexation," he coined what has become perhaps one of the foundational colonial phrases of U.S. history, *Manifest Destiny*. For O'Sullivan, Manifest Destiny gave the United States the "right" to "overspread and to possess the whole of our continent which Providence has given us for the development of the great experiment of liberty and federated self-government entrusted to us." O'Sullivan's coupling of expansion and democratic rights, of course, was not isolated to 1845.

Since the Northwest Ordinance of 1787, Americans had melded natural rights discourse with land expansionism. Indeed, since its founding moment, U.S. democracy was a spatial endeavor, created from the openness and vastness of the U.S. continent. O'Sullivan's phrase *Manifest Destiny* was not just timely because it documented the historical implications of coupling geographic expansionism with the "development of millions of democratic peoples." It also marked a moment of unprecedented territorial growth, when "frontier" land would become a documented reality for the U.S. masses. This was the period when the lands west of the Mississippi became part of the United States and were not merely understood as an abstract marker for democracy's expansive potential. By the end of this period, the United States had grown by 70 percent and was a transcontinental democracy, a nation whose boundaries went "from sea to shining sea." In this period, America realized its Manifest Destiny by annexing, conquering, and stealing lands of the West with the mission of promoting democracy. In many ways, the years surrounding O'Sullivan's creation of the phrases *Manifest Destiny* and *the Mexican Question* were defining modern moments in American documentality, a liminal period that would test the foundations of democracy and its territorial roots. For at the same time that the United States' geographical boundaries expanded, the nation questioned its new democratic mission of expansion. Two interrelated and fundamental questions took hold of American documentary culture: What "rights" did the United States have to annex Mexican lands? And could the norms and ideals of democracy such as rights of the people extend to these recently incorporated lands? O'Sullivan's essay "The Mexican Question," written within months of his coining of the term *Manifest Destiny*, dealt with both of these issues. "The Mexican Question" revealed both the rights-based language that fueled America's expansion and the anxiety that racial others and their lands created for U.S. democratic culture.

For O'Sullivan, "The Mexican Question" was primarily an inquest concerning the United States' "natural rights" to expand west, as well as which people—the Mexicans or the Americans—had the right to these lands. To this end, much as in "Annexation," in "The Mexican Question" O'Sullivan argued that Mexican lands enabled the free development of the American people. Important to his inquest was his exploration of how the United States could reconcile the concept of "natural rights" to give the United States a democratic justification to occupy Mexico's sovereign lands. His question was complicated by the fact that Mexicans were a distinct people who had created their own democratic government. In order for O'Sullivan to resolve the question of Mexico's sovereignty over their lands, he felt that the United States had to find that democracy could naturally extend to the western territories, that expansion was the providential natural right of the American people. Not surprisingly, O'Sullivan ultimately argued that the American people held the natural right to the lands. But what is interesting are the political maneuvers that he made in his essays to answer his own Mexican Question.

O'Sullivan merged a Lockean notion of individual natural rights with the rhetoric of Manifest Destiny and bestowed the sovereign nation and its collective people with the same natural rights as the individual in "nature." It is important to remember that natural rights are those that God bestows on individuals at birth; in secularized Lockean republicanism, natural rights are those that a person is born with in the state of nature. These "naturally" entail the right to life, liberty, and the pursuit of happiness. Then, following Jeffersonian Enlightenment rhetoric, O'Sullivan argued that rights were "naturally" rooted in the soil of the providential United States and thus were foundational to the development of peoplehood. Much like Jefferson, O'Sullivan considered the natural landscape to be the source of the democratic ideal of rights. O'Sullivan's coupling of individual rights and Manifest Destiny was finally dependent on the argument that Mexicans were not capable of "imagining" the concept of natural rights and peoplehood in the first place.

I cannot underscore enough to what extent the "Mexican Question" that emerged in O'Sullivan's *Democratic Review* set the documentary foundations for American and Mexican relations in the decades to come. First, the inquiry revealed how the United States came to terms with the expansion of a continent through an expanded notion of "natural rights" discourses and racial imperatives of domination over another sovereign democratic nation. Second, for O'Sullivan's and the nation's immediate manifest designs, the Mexican Question fueled the justification for a "rightful," "just" war against Mexico. Indeed, one year after O'Sullivan wrote "The Mexican Question" and "Annexation," the United States declared war against Mexico and began its "rightful expansion" into the West through force.

O'Sullivan was not alone in this argument: it appears in a number of essays in his publication, the *Democratic Review*. Perhaps the most striking essay to discuss the racial implications of the "Mexican Question" was "Mexico," written by the American expansionist and ardent supporter of republican ideologies Caleb Cushing. In this essay, Cushing begins by asserting that the Mexican Question is one that affects "the just estimation of our [America's] own rights" and concludes by affirming that the United States has the right to lands because of the remarkable racial differences between the two countries. In the United States, whites make up over "six-sevenths of the whole population," while only one-seventh of Mexico's population is made up of the European races. For Cushing, "race is the key to much that seems obscure in the history of a nation and its ability to foster a free and representative democracy." Since Mexico is mostly Indians and half-breeds, Cushing argues, Americans will look in "vain" for an "enlightened population."

In the end, natural law and rights-based arguments for expansion gave the U.S. people the moral justification to limit the freedoms of Mexico and the people of the West. The U.S.-Mexico War of 1846–48 solidified the spatial, racial, and democratic foundations of the Mexican Question in the United States. The war created geographic boundaries that expanded America's empire by more than a third and promoted racial stereotypes of Mexicans that affected Mexican and Anglo relations for generations. Moreover, the U.S.-Mexico War was the United States' first war on foreign soil and was arguably one of the most important landmarks in the development of American territory. For the young nation trying to define itself, the war helped promote republican ideals domestically, as well as demonstrating to a growing global economy that America modeled itself as a republic of destiny, one able to win a war with a foreign power.

As cultural historian Robert Johannsen argues, the Mexican War also played an important part in the breakdown of American parochialism: "It marked America's first intimate exposure to a life and culture that differed significantly from anything in the American experience. . . . The American people . . . would never be the same." As a consequence, however, the war and the Treaty of Guadalupe Hidalgo that ended it in 1848 would greatly challenge the rhetoric of the American public sphere and the political and racial identity of white Americans.

The military campaign against Mexico quickly led to the documentation of Mexican people as foreign and exotic in the public imagination. Occurring against a backdrop of American technological innovations, including the beginnings of widely circulated newspapers, magazines, and dime novels, the war touched more American lives than any other event in America's history up to that moment. The perception of Mexicans in the American imagination, however, was not flattering. The literary public spheres represented Mexicans as people who had "exotic and foreign manners" and a "darker phenotype," and who spoke an inferior language. These and other stereotypes inevitably constituted Mexicans as racially inferior in the minds of Anglo-Americans. Such a racial outlook inevitably helped promote the war effort. Indeed, to gain the support of the American public, the U.S. government used a number of propaganda techniques to cast negative stereotypes of Mexicans as a people in America's social imagination. Similar to the racial stereotypes that Lighton's "The Greaser" employed, Mexican people were rendered with specific embodied racial characteristics in the United States' emerging mass document culture. In other words, embodiment became the defining contour of the Mexican Question.

A widely publicized 1848 study undertaken by a Cincinnati phrenologist found that the Mexican people "were destitute of Comparison, Causality, Constructiveness, Ideality, and Benevolence, while they possessed in abundance Combativeness, Destructiveness, Secretiveness, and Acquisitiveness," and that "Mexicans' thick skulls" revealed that they were very coarse and more animal than intellectual.

The signing of the Treaty of Guadalupe Hidalgo on February 2, 1848, solidified these inquests through an act of government documentality. For this is the first document both to deal with the question of U.S. democracy's capacity to expand into the West and to establish, in natural rights theory, the newly documented political subject known as the "Mexican-American." The Treaty of Guadalupe Hidalgo is the first document to address the civil rights of Mexicans as an incorporated U.S. people. In theory, the treaty constituted Mexicans as American people endowed with the natural rights of Americans and the once-Mexican lands as U.S. public domain. At the same time that it geographically documented Mexican lands, borders, territories, and property rights, articles 8 and 9 granted Mexicans the legal right to be included in the body politic as "American citizens" and as property owners, while still maintaining their private traditions as Mexicans who were Spanish-speaking Catholics. However, as Martha Menchaca and Deena González have argued, the treaty only gave a semblance of democratic inclusion, natural rights, and land rights. Mexican-Americans' mixed-race background, Menchaca argues, historically placed them in an ambiguous racial and legal position in the public sphere. In effect, their private racial body collided with the universal imperatives of the democratic public and the abstract notions of natural rights that were so central to the United States' emerging document culture. At varying times in U.S. history, the nation's legal, political, and literary spheres documented Mexicans as white, mixed-blood, and racially other. This would drastically affect their rights for over a century. In the end, the treaty did not truly guarantee any civil or property rights for Mexicans. Indeed, because of various state ratifications of the treaty, the Land Act of 1851, and the Gadsden Purchase, Mexican-Americans found that the treaty did not guarantee any rights for them as an American people at all. This would have profound effects on their ability to self-document and to attain and maintain documents in the United States.

The U.S.-Mexico War and the treaty that followed set a contradictory precedent of documentality that would haunt both Anglo-Americans and Mexican-Americans from the ending of the war well through the twenty-first century. Gómez-Quiñones makes this point when he argues that the treaty would stand as a foundational civil rights document affecting not only how Anglos constitute Mexican-Americans as a people in documentary culture but also how Mexicans document themselves as private and public subjects of an American nation that first promised an "egalitarian" and "benevolent" solution to the war. Moreover, as Norma Alarcón astutely theorizes, the war and the treaty that followed "dichotomized" Mexicans in the United States as a split documented people, the "Mexican American." According to the contradictory document-making language of the treaty, the Mexicans' designation in the United States inked them as both strangers and members of the United States, and, as such, Mexican people in the United States have had to fight for their inclusion in the courts and in the literary and political public spheres as a dichotomized political specter.

In the social imaginary of the Anglo-American population in the United States, the Treaty of Guadalupe Hidalgo established a civil, racial, and geographic definition of Mexican documentality that would expedite Anglo incorporation of lands across the continent. None other than the progenitor of the nineteenth-century use of "specter," Karl Marx's comrade Friedrich Engels, captured the document-making importance of the treaty for American capitalist enterprise when he engaged in his own Mexican Question in the 1849 essay "Democratic Pan-Slavism":

> How did it happen that over Texas a war broke out between these two republics, which, according to moral theory, ought to have been "fraternally united" and "federated," and that, owing to "geographical, commercial and strategic necessities," the "sovereign will" of the American people, supported by the bravery of the American volunteers, shifted the boundaries drawn by nature some hundreds of miles further south? Or is it perhaps unfortunate that splendid California has been taken away from the lazy Mexicans, who could not do anything with it? That the energetic Yankees by rapid exploitation of the Californian gold mines will increase the means of circulation, in a few years will concentrate a dense population and extensive trade at the most suitable places on the coast of the Pacific Ocean, create large cities, open up communications by steamship, construct railways from New York to San Francisco, for the first time really open the Pacific Ocean to civilization, and the third time really open the Pacific to a new direction? The "independence" of a few Spanish Californians and Texans may suffer because of it; in some places "justice" and other moral principles may be violated; but what does that matter compared to such facts as world-historic significance.

For Engels and Marx, the implications of progress toward a Communist revolution outweighed any moral or ethical issues of war, geopolitical expansion, and the legal rhetoric of the aforementioned treaty that would "violate" the rights and status of Mexicans as a people. I want to point out that, like Lighton's racist rhetoric in "The Greaser," Marx's and Engels's arguments relied on racist justifications that the Mexican people were "lazy." In 1861, even Marx argued in a *New York Daily Tribune* article that Mexicans were "degenerate" and thus, in the end, they "rejoice in the conquest of Mexico," for Mexicans can learn from the "tutelage of the American people."

Not all Americans were completely sure that the Mexican people were capable of tutelage, however. Echoing the racial sentiments of Marx and Engels, Senator John C. Calhoun made a statement to Congress that was later printed in the *Congressional Record*; he stated that Mexicans represented "a motley amalgamation of impure races, not [even] as good as Cherokees and Choctaws." He went on to ask the American public if they could "incorporate a people so dissimilar in every respect—so little qualified for free and popular government—without certain destruction to our political institutions. We do not want the people of Mexico, either as citizens or subjects." Calhoun's comments about Mexicans found their impetus in his anxiet-ies about the United States' ability to "democratically" control the western territories and the newly documented Mexicans who lived on U.S. lands after the war. Discussing the limits and possibilities of American documentary culture the same year as Engels, 1849, Senator Calhoun asked if the "constitution extended to the territories or does it not extend to them." Calhoun's question reveals how the territorial growth of the United States after the signing of the treaty and the Gadsden Purchase of 1853 would generate foundational ques-tions about the capacity of democracy and its ability to deal with the new lands that it had forcefully acquired. Much like O'Sullivan in "The Mexican Question," in the end, Calhoun felt that democracy could deal with the new landscapes and the Mexicans, for the racial mission of the United States enabled him to declare that expansion and democracy were not contradictory; they were complementary. But how would they continue to document the Other in the future in order to maintain this colonial negotiation?

*

One hundred and fifty years later, the origins of the Mexican Question haunt me at night. Perhaps watching Alex Rivera's *Sleep Dealer* too often or the new dose of Lexapro leads me to have vivid dreams every night for a week while I apply to become a census taker for the 2020 census. I tried to get such a job ten years earlier but wasn't chosen. I am hoping to work neighborhoods where Latinxs, with the new SCOTUS decision, are at risk of being erased with new questions about their citizenship and race. The dream repeats itself in parts over a week while I wait for the interview. Though fleeting and partial, in every version of this dream I am a census taker in some near future and the skin of my entire body is translucent, like onionskin paper. Just under my epidermis lies a digitized map that warms my skin and yet is cold to the touch. Every morning before I begin my task of going door-to-door to ask questions, I stare at a mirror, naked, and map coordinates light up orange, yellow, green, and red just under my skin, which glows a blue hue. I try to rub it off my body, but my mind is distracted and taken over by echoing questions layered upon questions entering my head from someplace I think is on my body:

> *What is your name?*
> *Who are you?*
> *Where do you come from?*
> *Are you a citizen?*

In the next moment, I am taken to an apartment complex where my mom and I lived when we moved from Texas, the place in L.A. where, as a young boy, I met the librarian who introduced me to archives and the *Florentine Codex*. I am then going from door to door asking questions:

> *What is your name?*
> *Where do you come from?*
> *Are you a citizen?*

Their answers mark my body and the map inscribes or erases them with each answer. Most disappear after the last question. I come to a door and a young boy opens; it is me as a young boy; and, strangely, not shocked by my younger doppelganger, I ask myself the same question in every dream:

> *Who are you?*

It ends at that moment.

I don't take the job. I can't take the job. I can't become an agent of Mexican Questions, a body of inquiry. I also worry that the dreams will bring too much anxiety, bring about too many more questions. I am far too exhausted the next day after I have the dreams. Exhaustion leads to anxiety and anxiety to more Lexapro, which then leads to more dreams I can't comprehend. I think that if I resolve "who I am" these haunting dreams will go away. Perhaps this recent bout of anxiety will be alleviated. Three weeks later I take a DNA test (Geno 2.0), wondering if the ghosts lurking in the strands of my DNA will answer my questions. I spit into a test tube, hoping that this saliva sample will answer my Mexican Question once and for all. My inquiry is answered in six weeks with yet another document:

Southwestern Europe		48%
North America & Andes		27%
Northwestern Europe		8%
Italy & Southern Europe		4%
Southwest Asia/Persian Gulf		3%
Asia Minor		3%
Jewish Diaspora		2%
Northeastern Europe		2%
Western Africa		2%

The dream returns that night. But this time, after I ask the boy, "Who are you?" he hands me my DNA sequence. I read the first lines: 456-T—4768-0987-874903-43-65-87-TU-7-*-t-7 . . . but I am lost . . . I can't understand what the numbers mean, but my body begins to remap the numbers like coordinates:

"Is this who I am?"

It's just a dream, I tell myself over and over . . .

...the dream continues to haunt me. The DNA only leads to more questions, to a reality unmoored to any materiality. My Mexican Question unresolved. I hope that returning to the archives, perhaps to Bataille's base materialism, will help rectify my unconscious and disrupt the patterns of racialization that my mind can't escape. A warrant deep in the psyche that never concludes, an archive fever caught from the question of the colonized self, lost in an echoing batholith that looks like a brain. Here, deep in this caldera, I find Emma Tenayuca's grave and uncover her haunted writings.

The Mexican people's movement in the Southwest will constitute one more important and powerful link in the growing movement for the democratic front in the United States. The achievement of its objectives will be a decisive step forward toward the national unification of the American people.

-EMMA TENAYUCA, "THE MEXICAN QUESTION IN THE SOUTHWEST"-

She finds me in those anxious years I spent recovering every document and image that mentions the phrase "the Mexican Question," wondering if I would ever find a Mexican who engaged with this rhetoric in such blatant terms. For years, to my disappointment, I only recovered the white Americans who focused on documenting the Other in the first decades in which this inquiry emerged.

Their words, their questions about my documentality, my subjectivity, framed my understanding of self more than I realized. They had fashioned me into a self-doubting racial object of their inquiry. Their documents turned me into Lighton's Greaser, a savage of terra incognita, and Trump's Mexican Questions would only reconfirm this feeling with each racist speech I heard on the nightly news before I tried to sleep.

Am I a terrorist, a murderer, a Mexican rapist, an animal?

Working as a research fellow for the Recovering the U.S. Hispanic Literary Heritage project, an endeavor to locate all of the lost or erased documents written by Latinx peoples from colonialism to 1960, I wondered why I was even using my and their resources to recover the voices of racist Anglos. As one archive led to yet another archive, it started to make sense to me: Mexicans at that time weren't really going around questioning their ability to be documented in this form, or questioning what their rights and status were, when they had none; this inquiry was a question created by and for the colonist, not the colonized, who couldn't utter such a question in public. Among the thousands of recovered documents, Emma Tenayuca did answer this question for me. Maybe I would hear her radical call, embody her will to answer the questions that have framed us as Others for generations. Maybe for all of us who have been the object of this inquiry, buried within the archives, this radical Chicana answered our pleas to speak out from her resting place and revealed her work and life spent challenging the racist and masculine norms of documentality. Her pursuit and accomplishments have been buried not only by the colonial Mexican Questions but also by the Chicanos and radicals who erased her writings and activism from Chicanx history.

A political activist and organizer of the 1930s, Emma Tenayuca wrote the profoundly important though little-studied document titled "The Mexican Question in the Southwest," a radical Marxist manifesto that recovers an emancipatory language for the oppressive situation of undocumented and documented Mexicans in the United States. Her Mexican Question dreams of Mexican collectivity including both the undocumented and documented through a reformulation of the Marxist rhetoric espoused by the national Communist Party. As one of the first Chicana activists, and one who became the state secretary of the Communist Party, Tenayuca tried to come to terms with the place that Mexicans would hold, not only in the Communist Party but also within the borders of the United States. Her works reveal a desire to remix the radical philosophies of Marx, Stalin, and Lenin to create a collective Mexican people in the geographic region of the Southwest. In effect, she wanted to answer the Mexican Question in her own radical terms.

For Tenayuca, the heart of Mexican oppression is both the racial and the economic discrimination that originated with the imperialist U.S.-Mexico War, a war, she argues, that was motivated by both racial and geopolitical imperatives and split the Mexican people into two categories, the documented Mexicans of the Southwest and the undocumented immigrants. Among the many questions that the essay explores is whether or not Mexicans consist of separate geographic nations and peoples. She concludes that they do not, for all Mexicans, documented or undocumented, are linked economically to the Anglo-American working classes and spatially to the land by the founding document that constitutes all "Mexican-Americans," the Treaty of Guadalupe Hidalgo. In this way, she is, to a degree, in line with the populist rhetoric of the 1930s Left, which advocated in much milder terms for Mexicans to be considered part of the larger collective because of their class position as workers.

To be sure, Tenayuca breaks with party lines and Marxist populist rhetoric when she posits that Mexicans are a national minority who have a historical past and a relationship to the land that makes them a distinct people within the larger collective. Both the documented and undocumented are Mexican people first, as they share a collective history. After establishing that Mexicans are a distinct and unified people, however, she then proclaims that a collective Mexican people can effectively change the entire U.S. body politic: "The Mexican people's movement in the Southwest will constitute one more important and powerful link in the growing movement for the democratic front in the United States. The achievement of its objectives will be a decisive step forward toward the national unification of the American people."

Though not as blatantly radical as the seditionist 1915 document called the Plan de San Diego, Tenayuca's radicalism attempts to insert all Mexicans into the geopolitical imagination of the Marxist Left by first documenting them as a unified people with a shared colonial past. Only if Marxists embrace Mexicans as a distinct people with a documented history can Marxism exist as a viable discourse of minority peoplehood. In this way, Tenayuca echoes Kenneth Burke's ideas that we must focus on the ideal of the people and not solely the worker. For Tenayuca, however, the people are not invariable; they are not devoid of their particular historical and racial characteristics—they are the Mexican people, who have a long, documented history that can be traced to the Aztecs. Only if Marxism embraces their unique history and circumstances of imperialism in the Southwest will the populist dreams of Marxism become a materially viable popular front for Mexicans in the United States.

Tenayuca's "The Mexican Question in the Southwest" finds its roots in but also challenges a long line of Marxist thought and history relating to Mexicans. Certainly, it departs from Marx's spectral inquiry "On the

Jewish Question" (1847)—a manifesto that was the first to establish the dialectic between the universal worker and ethnic people. Unlike "On the Jewish Question" and a number of works that followed about the universal class collective, however, Tenayuca's question challenges the universal ideals set up in Marxist thought that turn race into a specter. It is particularly interesting that the Marxist roots and historical contradictions that Tenayuca's "The Mexican Question in the Southwest" reveals go back to the very same year that Marx wrote "On the Jewish Question." During the U.S.-Mexico War, Edgar von Westphalen, Karl Marx's brother-in-law, led a radical Marxist movement in none other than Texas in 1847. A member of the German Socialist Party and a part-time economic philosopher who exchanged ideas with Marx, von Westphalen went to Texas during the U.S.-Mexico War to create a utopian, not Mexican, community. It failed.

In contradistinction to Marxism's inability to deal with race, Tenayuca's "The Mexican Question" is trying to locate a radical thinking that will account for both the rights of racial others and economic emancipation. She tries to create a critical race Marxism that accounts for the relationship between these two important aspects of subjectivity and cultural formation. She responds to the Communist Party's race questions of the 1930s, specifically the "Negro Question," which posited that African Americans consisted of a separate nation in the United States, what many refer to as the "Black Belt thesis." She disagrees with this formulation because it creates a segregationist ideology within the popular front's thought. Again it is important to reiterate that Tenayuca's essay should also be read with and against the Anglo-American "Mexican Question" that emerged in the nineteenth century. According to Tenayuca, the "Mexican Question(s)" in Anglo-America concerning the documented rights and status of Mexicans—Who are the Mexican people? What is their race? What are their rights after the war? How will they affect "We, the People" of Anglo-America?—were all predicated on ideologies that emerged from struggles over the effect of documents on *all* Mexicans of Greater Mexico. To this end, Tenayuca wants to erase the Marxist rhetoric that defines Mexicans as a specter of the United States and inscribe them as a self-documenting people with a particular history and culture. Her lessons have yet to be realized.

*

FORJANDO EL DESTINO
For Emma Tenayuca

In the photo you are a young, impassioned speaker,
fist raised. I can hear your voice, loud and clear.
I ask, "What gave you the courage, Emma?"
I know the answer.

With youth's passion you fought injustice
fought for pecan shellers—women, young and old, and children too.

You worked alongside them
and smelled the acrid smell
and felt the stifling heat
and the dust covered your hands and your hair
in spite of the scarf you wore
and you heard them cough
and you laughed with them
and you cried with them
until it was time to say no more
no more to wage cuts
no more to unsafe conditions.

Time for the struggle to begin.
Time for destiny to carry you on its wings.
You had a gift. And you used it.
Others followed. Twelve thousand workers walked away
from poorly paid jobs
and the bosses had to listen
and the papers had to cover the story
and you won. And lost.
Had to go on your way.
Destiny led you to California, away from the ex-husband,
away from the embarrassed relatives,
the nosy neighbors,
the prying reporters.
And destiny brought you back
a teacher,
a shaper of young minds,
to sustain language and culture,
fighting injustice in another terrain.

Your razor-sharp mind never at rest, always working,
always thinking. The words and the thoughts almost
too much. The books, the papers, your work.

Honor and glory came late;
your memory lives in the hearts of those who knew you,
those who never met you but honor your passion
and join you in the struggle still not won.

¡Adelante!
—*Norma Cantú*—

I am nostalgic for sleep, so I hang the portrait of Emma Tenayuca with
Norma Cantú's poem underneath. I try to imagine myself as a radi-
cal, as a person answering, with fist raised, all the racist rhetoric sur-
rounding the Mexican Question, which has documented my identity
for generations before me. I can't find any steps high enough. I am left
with the specter of radicalism buried in archives that I intellectualize
from afar and these damn nightmares. I close my eyes, and I see her
grave and read her tombstone: "Thy will be done . . ."

BOOK VI
Rhetoric and Moral Philosophy

Savage and Decadent

eyes

wise

and humble

Cruel virtues

contained

In life

we

invent

language

of

ancestors

HOMO DOCUMENTATOR

These people won't exist unless they're documented!

-RAMIRO GOMEZ, ARTIST-

WHO . . . WHAT IS A DOCUMENT?

Aztecs made *amatl* paper two hundred years before they were turned into a document by the Spaniards. At the time when this "paper world" emerged before the conquest, Aztecs were making over twenty-four thousand reams annually to use in rituals, to make books, and for acts of necropoetics. The *Florentine Codex* related that paper was burned to ward off illness and stave off death. Not only was paper used to help the living fight death but, when death was inevitable, *amatl* helped them mediate their journey to the underworld, as their bodies were adorned with paper when they died. Their burial place even included a jar full of paper so they could negotiate between life and death, described as being "between two mountain ranges, which are joining with one another." Scholar Victor Wolfgang von Hagen argues that the paper world created by the Aztecs before the conquest was much more advanced than the paper worlds created by their European conquerors.

The making of this "paper world" was a time-consuming art. It started with the cutting of the *amatl* bark, a task traditionally performed by men, while the further processing was mostly up to the women. Cutting the bark requires a special know-how; the different tree species have their own cutting seasons depending on their growth cycle. The process performed on *amatl* trees in Pahuatlán, Puebla, was the following: They are macerated in water and left to soften overnight in streams and rivers. Then they are boiled in ash-water or lime-water (also used in nixtamalizing corn to make tortillas). This process takes several hours and may be repeated. The fibers of the inner bark (bast)—separated from the exterior parts—are softened. Once the bark is stripped off and the exterior part has been cleaned, it is stretched out and thinned by being pounded with a flat stone; it is slashed with a few striations and then beaten with a willow branch doubled over into a circle, like a handle. It is then cut into long strips, which are beaten again with another flatter stone and polished, and finally it is split into leaves two spans long and about a span and a half wide. The fiber pulp is arranged on a wooden board in the form of a grid, and then beaten and felted with a stone, the so-called *machacador*. The beaten upper side is somewhere between rough and smooth, like the bark of an aspen tree. Then it is further pressed and flattened. The last step is to stretch the paper in frames and dry it in the hot sun. The final product is very similar to thick, smooth poster-board paper, but more compact and whiter.

The conquest found its foothold when the Spaniards burned thousands of Mesoamerican books and reams of paper. In doing so, they turned the paper world of the Aztecs to ash that smelled of sweet bark. Colonialism and its twin brother the Enlightenment turned *amatl* paper into a state document and alienated and reified the paper maker's sacred necropoetic act into one created by and for the conquest of the Other, an act of cataloguing their existence in the nation-state with pulp and pixels. Colonialism turned necropoetics into necropolitics.

There is no document of civilization which is not at the same time a document of barbarism.

A document [now] is an inscribed [colonial] act.... In the framework I am proposing, a document should be understood rather as something that is given once and for all and as making up a class of stable objects, as the reification of social acts which, in turn, change over time and space. What is constant here is not the kind of act in question nor the documents that follow from them, but rather the fact that without acts and without inscriptions, no society is conceivable.

Because nothing social exists outside the text, papers, archives, and documents constitute the fundamental elements of the social world. Society is not based on communication but on registration, which is the condition for the creation of social objects. Human beings grow as human beings and socialize through registration.

Naked life is nothing but a remote starting point, and culture begins very early making for a clothed life, which is manifested in registrations and imitations: languages, behaviors, and rites. This explains why writing is so important, and, even more, "archinscription," which is the realm of registration that precedes and includes writing in its proper or current meaning. As regards a theory of mind, social ontology is based on ichnology, which is to say a theory of traces (it is important to distinguish ichnology as the science of traces from ichnology as a branch of geology).

The representation of the mind as a tabula or a writing surface is not a mere metaphor, but captures the fact that perceptions and thoughts come to us as inscriptions in our mind. But the mind is not just an inscribed surface, it is also capable of grasping inscriptions, namely the traces that there are in the world, on the surface that is before us in experience.

We can make out an ascending hierarchy that takes in traces (any incision on a background), registrations (traces in the mind as a tabula*) and inscriptions in the technical sense (traces available to at least two persons).*

Documents can have practical purposes or they can be mainly directed to the evocation of sentiments. In the latter case, we have artworks, understood as those entities that pretend to be persons. Historians tell us that the word documentation *was coined by the American Documentation Institute at its founding in 1937 to connote the joining of new information technologies with a universalist rationalist philosophical outlook.*

A document—be it a book or a cash register receipt—is something that preserves someone's thoughts or ideas, or some bit of information that would otherwise be carried away by the river of time. . . . What are documents? They are, quite simply, talking things. They are bits of the material world—clay, stone, animal skin, plant fiber, sand—that we've imbued with the ability to speak. To say that documents speak is perhaps to indulge in poetic license, which might be avoided by simply saying that they represent or communicate and leaving it at that. But to do this would be to lose the elegant and suggestive parallel between documents and people. Like all parallels, this one is incomplete and inexact. If it is useful, however, it will not be because documents and people are exactly the same, but because their similarities and their differences are illuminating, because the partial parallel sheds light on what documents are and perhaps also on what we humans are.

Documentation is a set of techniques developed to manage significant (or potentially significant) documents, meaning, in practice, printed texts. But there was (and is) no theoretical reason why documentation should be limited to texts, let alone printed texts. There are many other kinds of signifying objects in addition to printed texts. And if documentation can deal with texts that are not printed, could it not also deal with documents that are not texts at all? How extensively could documentation be applied? Stated differently, if the term "document" were used in a specialized meaning as the technical term to denote the objects to which the techniques of documentation could be applied, how far could the scope of documentation be extended. What could (or could not) be a document? The question was, however, rarely formulated in these terms.

Document: Any source of information, in material form, capable of being used for reference or study or as an authority.

Examples: manuscripts, printed matter, illustrations, diagrams, museum specimens, etc. . . . The antelope as document: Briet enumerates six objects and asks if each is a document. Object—Document? Star in sky—No; Photo of star—Yes; Stone in river—No; Stone in museum—Yes; Animal in wild—No; Animal in zoo—Yes. There is discussion of an antelope. An antelope running wild on the plains of Africa should not be considered a document, she rules. But if it were to be captured, taken to a zoo and made an object of study, it has been made into a document. It has become physical evidence being used by those who study it.

We infer, however, from her discussion that: (1) there is materiality: physical objects and physical signs only; (2) there is intentionality: it is intended that the object be treated as evidence; (3) the objects have to be processed: they have to be made into documents; and, we think, (4) there is a phenomenological position: the object is perceived to be a document. This situation is reminiscent of discussions of how an image is made art by framing it as art. Did Briet mean that just as "art" is made art by "framing" (i.e., treating) it as art, so an object becomes a "document" when it is treated as a document—i.e., as a physical or symbolic sign, preserved or recorded, intended to represent, to reconstruct, or to demonstrate a physical or conceptual phenomenon? The sources of these views are not made clear, though she does mention in this context her friend Raymond Bayer, a professor of philosophy at the Sorbonne, who specialized [in] aesthetics and phenomenology.

A document is the repository of an expressed thought. Consequently, its contents have a spiritual character. The danger that blunt unification of the outer form exercises a repercussion on the contents in making the latter characterless and impersonal is not illusory.... In standardizing the form and layout of documents it is necessary to restrict this activity to that which does not affect the spiritual contents ...

A document is something that is able to endure self-identically through time. It can be signed and countersigned, stored, registered, inspected, conveyed, copied, ratified, nullified, stamped, forged, hidden, lost or destroyed. Pluralities of documents can be chained together (for example, to form audit trials), and combined in other ways to form new document-complexes, whose structures mirror underlying human relations, for example of debtor to creditor, of manager to shareholder, of customer to supplier, of claimant to adjudicator, of doctor to patient, and so on. Documents thereby make possible new kinds of enduring social relations and new kinds of enduring social entities together allowing the evolution of entire new dimensions of socioeconomic reality. The effect is that private memory traces inside human brains are prosthetically augmented by publicly accessible documents and associated document technologies.

As these new documentary practices bring also changes in social relations, including changes in legal and economic systems, they bring into being new social artifacts, such as receipts, money, identity documents, criminal records, as well as signatures, document templates (to be filled in), check-boxes, official stamps, bank accounts, contracts, stocks, shares, mortgages, liens, insurance policies, credit cards, and so forth. The development of such artifacts and of the networks of social behavior and of claims and obligations with which are they associated is then in some ways analogous to the processes of biological evolution.

To be governed is to be under surveillance, inspected, spied on, superintended, legislated, regulated, restrained, indoctrinated, preached at, controlled, appraised, assessed, censored, commanded. . . . To be governed is to be noted, registered, enumerated, accounted for, stamped, measured, classified, audited, patented, licensed, authorized, endorsed, reprimanded, prevented, reformed, rectified, and corrected, in every operation, every transaction, every moment.

The creation of a "legible people," in James Scott's phrase—a people open to the scrutiny of officialdom—has become a hallmark of modern statehood; conversely, the mechanisms by which this has been achieved on a universal scale, that is, the paraphernalia and personnel necessary to operate systems of standardized registration, have contributed in large part to the character of the modern bureaucratic state. And not only the state: private economic and commercial activities would also grind to a halt unless companies had the ability to identify and track individuals as property owners, employees, business partners, and customers.

One set of questions that seems especially challenging at this stage is the relationship between emancipatory and repressive aspects of identity documentation. Registration and documentation of individual identity are essential if persons are to "count" in a world increasingly distant from the face-to-face encounters characteristic of less complex societies. Identity papers are at one and the same time papers of constraint and control, including control by the state, but they are also purveyors of identity. For each and every one of us our identity—at least a certain kind of identity—is enacted and reenacted, stamped, and affirmed in these papers. The identity document purports to be a record of uniqueness, but it also has to be an element in a classifying series, and it is thus simultaneously deindividualizing. This discloses the fundamental instability of the concept of the "individual" as such, and helps to explain the uneasy sense that we never fully own or control our identity, that the identity document carries a threat of expropriation at the same time that it claims to represent who we "are."

*

Show me your papers?

WHAT IS SB4 AND HOW DOES IT AFFECT ME?

 Texas' new "Show Me Your Papers" law allows law enforcement to ask people to prove their immigration status, increasing the potential for racial profiling targeting people of color.

 SB4 forces local law enforcement to comply with ICE holds, under the threat of criminal punishment. This undermines faith in law enforcement among the immigrant community.

 A fight over SB4 is a fight for the future: if it goes unchallenged, other states will pass similar laws. With bills pending in other states, *it's important to stand with Texas' immigrants!*

TEXT **WERISE** TO **698-66** TO SUPPORT TEXAS' IMMIGRANTS!

FOR America

TEXAS HOUSE OF REPRESENTATIVES

EDDIE RODRIGUEZ   FIFTY-FIRST DISTRICT

For Immediate Release: May 7, 2017
Contaçt: Alejandro Peña
(651) 491-5503; AlejandroD.Pena@house.texas.gov

GOVERNOR ABBOTT SIGNS SB 4,
"SHOW ME YOUR PAPERS" BECOMES LAW
SB 4 has been signed into law, to take effect September 1, 2017.

Austin, Texas - Today, Governor Greg Abbott signed Senate Bill 4 into law. SB 4 is the controversial "sanctuary cities" ban that the Texas Legislature passed last week. SB 4's "show me your papers" provision allows police to ask people their legal status after they have been detained or arrested. Instances of detainment include routine traffic stops.

State Rep. Eddie Rodriguez serves a district in Travis County, which has been at the center of the national "sanctuary cities" debate; on the House Committee of State Affairs, which removed the "show me your papers" provision before it was restored in the Texas House of Representatives; and as Policy Chair of the Mexican American Legislative Caucus, the oldest and largest Latino legislative caucus in the United States.

State Rep. Eddie Rodriguez issued the following statement regarding SB 4 being signed into law:
"Texas has its own 'show me your papers' law, thanks to Governor Greg Abbott.

"SB 4 will be challenged in court - you can take that to the bank. When Governor Abbott signed SB 4 tonight, he also signed a blank check on the taxpayer's' behalf to protect yet another blatantly discriminatory law.

"The law won't take effect until September 1, 2017. In the meantime, we must raise awareness about SB 4 so that folks are vigilant about racial profiling.

"Houston Police Chief Art Acevedo recently announced a 42% decrease in the number of Hispanic victims reporting rape to his department, and this 'chilling effect' is likely to get worse under SB 4. We must also empower all women who are victims of sexual violence to report their experiences and ensure that our laws aren't exploited by abusers.

"My colleagues and I in the Mexican American Legislative Caucus will not stop fighting against this law. We are the oldest and largest Latino caucus in the nation, and we will oppose SB 4 long after many of those who voted for its passage lose their seats in the Texas Legislature."

###

*

Is a document a person, a person a document?

STATE OF TEXAS

TEXAS DEPARTMENT OF HEALTH
BUREAU OF VITAL STATISTICS

UN/Documented

1. Not recorded or to provide documents
2. "illegal" immigrants
3. 11.6 million undocumented in US, 2015

TEXAS DEPARTMENT OF HEALTH
REC'D SEP 10 1969
BUREAU OF VITAL STATISTICS

CERTIFICATE OF BIRTH   BIRTH NO. 142-69 100760

OF TEXAS	2. USUAL RESIDENCE OF MOTHER [Where does mother live?]
COUNTY Harris	a. STATE Texas b. COUNTY Harris
TY OR TOWN [If outside city limits, give precinct no.]	c. CITY OR TOWN [If outside city limits, give precinct no.] Pasadena
Pasadena	d. STREET ADDRESS [If rural, give location] 2734 Lilac
Pasadena Memorial Hospital	e. IS RESIDENCE INSIDE CITY LIMITS? YES ☑ NO ☐ f. IS RESIDENCE ON A FARM? YES ☐ NO ☒

Mexican Surname

| (a) First John | 4a. THIS BIRTH | Michael [c] Last Rivera | 4. DATE OF BIRTH 7-2-69 |
| Male | SINGLE ☒ TWIN ☐ TRIPLET ☐ | 5. IF TWIN OR TRIPLET, WAS CHILD BORN 1st ☐ 2nd ☐ 3rd ☐ |

part of Mexico until 1848

Johnnie (None)	10. BIRTHPLACE [State or foreign country] Texas	Rivera	White ?
22 YEARS	12. USUAL OCCUPATION Airman Basic	11b. KIND OF BUSINESS OR INDUSTRY U.S. Air Force
Yolanda (None)	15. BIRTHPLACE [State or foreign country] Texas	Perez	White ?
21 YEARS	16. CHILDREN PREVIOUSLY BORN TO THIS MOTHER [Do not include this child] a. How many OTHER children are now living? -0-	b. How many OTHER children were born alive but are now dead? 0	c. How many children were born dead [fetal deaths after 20 weeks pregnancy]? 0

Paula Rivera

19a. ATTENDANT'S SIGNATURE
19c. ATTENDANT'S ADDRESS   N. L. Powers, M.D.
4040 Red Bluff Rd. Pasadena, Texas
20b. DATE REC'D BY LOCAL REGISTRAR 8-12-69
19b. ATTENDANT AT BIRTH M.D. ☒ D.O. ☐ MIDWIFE ☐ OTHER ☐
19d. DATE SIGNED 7-3-69
20c. REGISTRAR'S SIGNATURE W.C. Mays

On this date 540,000 Mexicans were defined as "undocumented"

This is to certify that this is a true and correct reproduction of the original record as recorded in this office. Issued under authority of Rule 54a, Article 4477, Revised Civil Statutes of Texas.

on this date 2.2 million Mexicans defined as "undocumented"

ISSUED OCT 2 3 1985

W.D. Carroll
W. D. CARROLL
STATE REGISTRAR

WARNING: IT IS ILLEGAL TO DUPLICATE THIS COPY. Be Mexican

CERTIFICATION OF VITAL RECORD

DEAD LANGUAGE

Some Coyotes are saying
that we Nahuas will disappear, will vanish,
our language will be heard no more,
will be used no more.
The Coyotes rejoice in this,
is this what they are looking for?
Why is it that they want us to disappear?
We do not have to contemplate this too long, because
four hundred years have shown us the aim of the Coyotes.
They are envious of our lands,
our forests and rivers,
our work, our sweat.

-UNKNOWN NAHUATL AUTHOR, *NAHUA MACEHUALPAQUILIZTLII*-

The concept of a dead language bespeaks the colonial hand that cuts off the tongue.

*

Sahagún began his first project, the *Primeros memoriales* and the *Psalmodia christiana*, as a dictionary that would forever document the Nahuatl language. He writes that he was made aware of the slow death of the Nahuatl language with every breath lost as millions perished. His work was in vain. Today, despite 1.5 million speakers in central Mexico, Nahuatl is an endangered language because most Mexicans speak Spanish as their main language.

*

Here in the United States I go to the ATM and am given the choice of reading the screen in English or Spanish. I choose English. I always choose English. I speak Baptist tongues, a gift from summers in Texas with my "charismatic" family, better than I do Spanish. Ostracized by the L.A. school district when I was in elementary school, my mom was told not to speak Spanish to me. My teacher, Mrs. Getz, told me that if I speak English, I have a better chance of getting a good job. Her advice and their lessons were complete. I lost my Spanish tongue by the time I was twelve. I became a professor of English and ensured it would never grow back.

*

The government still creates documents to erase tongues.

115TH CONGRESS
1ST SESSION

H. R. 997

To declare English as the official language of the United States, to establish
a uniform English language rule for naturalization, and to avoid mis-
constructions of the English language texts of the laws of the United
States, pursuant to Congress' powers to provide for the general welfare
of the United States and to establish a uniform rule of naturalization
under article I, section 8, of the Constitution.

IN THE HOUSE OF REPRESENTATIVES

FEBRUARY 9, 2017

Mr. KING of Iowa (for himself, Mr. COLLINS of Georgia, Mr. GOHMERT, Mr.
BARLETTA, Mr. DUNCAN of South Carolina, and Mr. FRANKS of Arizona)
introduced the following bill; which was referred to the Committee on
Education and the Workforce, and in addition to the Committee on the
Judiciary, for a period to be subsequently determined by the Speaker, in
each case for consideration of such provisions as fall within the jurisdic-
tion of the committee concerned

A BILL

To declare English as the official language of the United
States, to establish a uniform English language rule for
naturalization, and to avoid misconstructions of the
English language texts of the laws of the United States,
pursuant to Congress' powers to provide for the general
welfare of the United States and to establish a uniform
rule of naturalization under article I, section 8, of the
Constitution.

BOOK VII
The Sun, Moon, and Stars, and the Binding of the Years

My, Our   writings

      invented

The sun

                        The moon

        The Air

              The stars   The land

   The fire

Originated

                  In blindness

                         Language
                     the last element

                     translated whole

SANTA MUERTE (SAINT DEATH, SAINT OF THE DISPOSSESSED)

Poderosa Santa Muerte
En este día, dame paz,
Sabiduría y fuerza

-ORACIÓN A LA SANTA MUERTE-

Memento mori (Latin: "remember [that] you will die") is the medieval Latin Christian theory and practice of reflection on mortality, especially as a means of considering the vanity of earthly life and the transient nature of all earthly goods and pursuits. It is related to the **ars moriendi** *("The Art of Dying") and similar Western literature. Memento mori has been an important part of ascetic disciplines as a means of perfecting the character by cultivating detachment and other virtues, and by turning the attention towards the immortality of the soul and the afterlife.*

-WIKIPEDIA-

In reality when we curse death, we only fear ourselves.

-GEORGES BATAILLE-

Everything has its time. If I take death into my life, acknowledge it, and face it squarely, I will free myself from the anxiety of death and the pettiness of life—and only then will I be free to become myself.

-MARTIN HEIDEGGER, *BEING AND TIME*-

We know it is true
that we must perish,
for we are mortal men.
You, the Giver of Life,
you have ordained it.

We wander here and there
in our desolate poverty.
We are mortal men.

We have seen bloodshed and pain
where once we saw beauty and valor.

-AZTEC, ANONYMOUS, 1520-

*

I took a pilgrimage to Hollywood to reconcile with death. This journey, a long time delayed, found its first steps after a recent visit to the ER. My heart palpitations, known as PVCs (premature ventricular contractions), returned so badly that they did not stop for an hour. Worrying that I was having a heart attack, I went to the emergency room, where, after hours of tests, I was told by an attending PA, "You could be panicking about death and causing the rhythm of your heart to pause. They are normal and benign." The emergency doctors I was under the eye of found only one PVC in five hours:

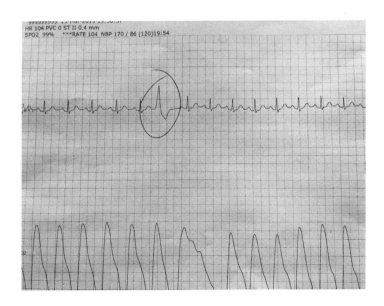

During the follow-up, my primary doctor concluded the same thing. Adrenaline from anxiety was racing to my heart and causing it to pause, a "sinus pause." Fear caused by the momentary skipping of a heartbeat makes me think for that instantaneous moment that it will not keep beating. That it will stop. For me, that feeling, that pause, is my memento mori, the moment I am confronted with its meaning: "Remember you must (will) die." It paralyzes me to such an extent that I do not live for the day, the moment, but rather I live in fear of when it will happen again, and, in doing so, I find myself losing my life to fear—fear of a future action my heart may or may not take; fear of a future PVC, which then leads to anxiety, which, in turn, then leads to more PVCs. The circle of memento mori. The doctor tries to reassure me with the ECG of my heart: "Look at it, let's read it together. You have to realize that it is normal. Benign. You can feel the skipped heartbeats while most cannot. Stop thinking about death and you will be fine. In the meantime, I am putting you on five milligrams of Lexapro. It works for you, right? But be aware one of the side effects of Lexapro is skipped heartbeats."

*

Four days later I find myself standing in the Templo Santa Muerte, a small hundred-square-foot room full of memento mori altars devoted to Saint Death. Santa Muerte is a powerful incarnation that finds its roots in the long history of Mexico's engagement with death. As Claudio Lomnitz has so thoroughly argued in his book *Death and the Idea of Mexico*, death is a framing discourse of Mexico's national and cultural identity, for both good and bad. Santa Muerte, then, is part of a long continuum of engagement with death in Mexico. Some argue that Santa Muerte finds its origins in the Aztec goddess of death, Mictecacihuatl. But there are a number of death saints that have inspired the modern belief in Santa Muerte, including a female death saint portrayed in Fray Joaquín Bolaños's novel *La portentosa vida de la Muerte* (1792), which was banned by the church. Santa Muerte, arguably, is an amalgamation and modern culmination of Mexico's necropolitics. The rituals associated with Santa Muerte can be traced to 1965 in Mexico City; by 2001 nearly 5 percent of all Mexicans prayed to the goddess of the dispossessed for protection. Some estimates put the number of practitioners of Santa Muerte, in one form or another, in the millions. Though devotees give offerings and pray to Santa Muerte, most remain Catholic. The Catholic church, however, has designated in "holy documents" that Santa Muerte is a Satanic cult; its embrace of an icon of death is discordant with key teachings of the Catholic church—namely, that Jesus conquered death and his resurrection is what gave birth to the church. Thus, to practice the rituals associated with Santa Muerte is sacrilegious and blasphemous. The U.S. and Mexican governments have also condemned the faith as being tied to criminality and drug cartels and have begun to destroy and put under surveillance certain "suspect" temples. Theologians too have argued that the faith, though the fastest growing among Mexicans in Mexico and the United States, has the makings of the occult.

Despite the attacks on the faith, immigrants in the United States have brought Santa Muerte with them from Mexico, and today there are now eleven temples or churches in the L.A. area. For its followers, Santa Muerte "represents a very real enemy to the power of death as a negative force." By praying to Santa Muerte, the undocumented and Latinx communities are able to fight the powers of the state that dictate life and death. Many undocumented even pray to Santa Muerte for green cards to help them become documented and for protection from ICE. This is why Santa Muerte has risen tremendously among those who are marginalized in communities, including those in LGBTQ+ communities in Mexico and the United States. By embracing death, the devotees of Santa Muerte challenge the state's ability to control death and its documents.

I go to the oldest temple in L.A., the Templo Santa Muerte in Hollywood, hoping that I can come to understand how death is embraced by undocumented and marginalized people and not feared, what Heidegger calls the condition of "Being-toward-death" (*Sein zum Tode*). Will it work for me? I do not look to put my faith in the Saint of Death but rather to come to terms with what it means to acknowledge death as a vital part of life, as a living symbol that guides you rather than paralyzes you with fear—or, in my case, makes your heart skip beats. Will Santa Muerte help me confront the phrase "remember you must die" with vigor or will death continue to paralyze me?

I have to admit to myself, I am a tourist. My life in Colorado is so distant from the death traditions that frame Mexico's sovereignty and culture. I question if this Saint of the Dispossessed and Undocumented will help a documented *pocho*. I walk two blocks on Melrose from the famed Paramount Studios to the Templo Santa Muerte. The building is small and has two claustrophobic rooms. To the left is a store where thousands of memento mori are for sale to help the devotee practice Santa Muerte at home. To the right is the temple. I enter the store, where a middle-aged woman in a long huipil greets me. "Can I help you?" "I am just looking," I tell her. She smiles and leaves the room. She lets me wander alone. I am overwhelmed by the smell of burning lavender and hemp and the hundreds of memento mori that line the floor, walls, and ceiling, creating a dizzying presence of death. The majority of the memento mori and altars that line the shelves are icons of a skeleton dressed in a long ornate gown. The skeleton's head is adorned with a gold-jeweled crown, and in her right hand she holds a large gold sickle. In the large statues, her right hand cradles a globe of the earth. She reminds me of the Virgen de Guadalupe, but in skeletal form. In the store there are hundreds of them for sale, along with key chains, shirts, and large rugs, all decorated in fine detail and made in Mexico.

I enter the temple to the right, which is guarded with a large metal gate, where I am confronted with hundreds of aged Santa Muerte altars. Some are small but most large, about four feet tall, and nearly all of them have under them small offerings of fruit, money, and small pieces of folded paper with requests. The woman walks from behind the altars and tells me to make an offering. "What?" I ask her. "Whatever you feel comfortable with," she says. I grab a scrap of paper and write in English, "Help me stop fearing death." I fold it and say a Hail Mary under my breath, a prayer that is ingrained in my psyche and has haunted me in its own way since my confirmation, before I set the paper down in the large wooden *molcajete*. I cannot give myself over to saying the prayer:

"Poderosa Santa Muerte
En este día, dame paz,
Sabiduría y fuerza."

My Catholic guilt prevents me from fully embracing Santa Muerte because I fear the church's doctrines against putting our faith in false gods and altars. The first step in my journey to reconcile with death is a failure. My past continues to haunt me despite its failing me for so many years. The PVCs return the day I land back in Colorado.

THE PICKING DEAD

For one hundred years succeeding waves of immigrants have sweated and sacrificed to make this industry rich. And for their sweat and for their sacrifice, farm workers have been repaid with humiliation and contempt. With all these problems, why, then, do we dwell so on the perils of pesticides? If we ignored pesticide poisoning—if we looked on as farm workers and their children are stricken—then all the other injustices our people face would be compounded by an even more deadly tyranny.

-ADDRESS BY CÉSAR CHÁVEZ, PRESIDENT, UNITED FARM
WORKERS OF AMERICA, AFL-CIO, AT PACIFIC LUTHERAN
UNIVERSITY, TACOMA, WASHINGTON, MARCH 1989-

Farmworkers are exposed to pesticides in a variety of ways. Workers who per-form hand labor tasks in treated areas risk exposure from direct spray, aerial drift, or contact with pesticide residues on the crop or soil. Workers who mix, load, or apply pesticides can be exposed to pesticides due to spills, splashes, and defective, missing, or inadequate protective equipment. Even when not working in the fields, farmworker families, especially children, are also at risk of elevated pesticide ex-posure. Workers bring pesticides into their homes in the form of residues on their tools, clothes, shoes, and skin. They inadvertently expose their children through a hug if they cannot shower after work. The close proximity of agricultural fields to residential areas results in aerial drift of pesticides into farmworkers' homes, schools, and playgrounds. Some schoolyards are directly adjacent to fields of crops that are sprayed with pesticides. Pesticide exposure is an unavoidable reality for farmworkers and their families because pesticides are in the air they breathe, the water they drink, the food they eat, and the soil they cultivate.

-FARMWORKER JUSTICE, *EXPOSED AND IGNORED: HOW PESTICIDES ARE ENDANGERING OUR NATION'S FARMWORKERS*-

Watching a thirty-eight-minute video created by PERC (Pesticide Educational Resources Collaborative) is as close as I get to understand-ing the perils of working the fields as an undocumented laborer while pesticides are sprayed on your back. After I watch it, I am supposed to understand the hazards of working with toxins and am certified to pick the fields in the United States. I ask my mom and grandmother if there were any videos for them to watch before they picked cotton in the fields of El Campo, Texas. "Videos? No videos." All they tell me is how hard it was, and how hundreds of cuts on your hands and legs were created by the saw briers that were in the fields and the bolls that held the cotton. The fields still haunt my family both in their memories and in their bodies. They suffer from the poisons that were sprayed on them for years. My dad and grandfather have lupus and scleroderma, my mom has Raynaud's disease and breast cancer, and my aunts have early onset rheumatoid arthritis. The poisons around my grandfather slowly killed him. I watched him slowly deteriorate over the summers, as his fingers lost all feeling, turning white as a ghost's sheet, a sad and horrible way to go for a man who escaped the fields to learn a trade and eventually made the space suits for NASA's Apollo missions. Though my family were able to escape the fields, go to college, earn PhDs, learn trades, the pesticides will haunt them forever, emerging as illnesses with no cures.

*

Doctors won't do it. Most physicians farm workers see won't even admit their patients' problems are caused by pesticides. They usually blame symptoms on skin rashes and heat stroke. Doctors don't know much about pesticides; the signs and symptoms of acute pesticide poisoning are similar to other illnesses. Doctors who work for growers or physicians with close ties to rural communities won't take a stand.

-CÉSAR CHÁVEZ, ADDRESS AT PACIFIC LUTHERAN UNIVERSITY-

My grandfather's illness went undiagnosed for years; so did my mother's and father's, and, I suspect, the illnesses of millions of other pickers who work the fields in this country. For decades doctors neglected to ask them if they picked and whether they were sprayed with pesticides. Would it have mattered? Most still argue that there is no direct relationship between picking and autoimmune diseases, between picking and illnesses that slowly kill you years after your body has long succumbed to the backbreaking work of picking.

My daughter shows me the white of her toes and tells me she cannot feel them when they are cold. "Dad, I have Raynaud's disease like grandmother. How can I have this? I didn't pick like them." We take my daughter to the doctor, where she is given a number of blood tests. At the consultation, the doctor tells us the results are inconclusive. "Can autoimmune diseases run in the family?" I ask her. I tell the doctor that autoimmune diseases run in our family, and especially the relatives from El Campo and the ones who picked. "Is it in our genes? I don't have a disease yet," I tell her. She says that it is inconclusive whether pesticides cause cancer and autoimmune diseases, but they could be a contributing factor. "How about Elyse?" I ask. "Maybe it's in our genes now? Can pesticide poisoning skip a generation . . . can picking in the fields continue to affect and even haunt the bodies of future generations?" The doctor looks at me like I am crazy. "There is no science for that," she says. "Today there isn't, but is anyone looking?" I ask.

DAY OF THE DEAD©

The applicant, Disney Enterprises, Inc., a corporation of
Delaware, having an address of 500 South Buena Vista
Street, Burbank, California 91521, United States, requests
registration of the trademark / service mark identified above
in the United States Patent and Trademark Office on the
Principal Register established by the Act of July 5, 1946 (15
U.S.C. Section 1051 et seq.), as amended, for the following:
International Class 041: Education and entertainment ser-
vices. Intent to Use: The applicant has a bona fide intention
to use or use through the applicant's related company or
licensee the mark in commerce on or in connection with the
identified goods and/or services. (15 U.S.C. Section 1051(b)).

A fee payment in the amount of $325 has been submitted with the application, representing payment for 1 class(es).

Addendum:

*All ten (10) Disney TM applications for DIA DE LOS MUERTOS were voluntarily abandoned . . . they never received TM registration.

*Disney applied for the trademarks to own Day of the Dead on May 7, 2013; the story was broken on CNN on May 10, 2013, and Disney filed to voluntarily abandon the applications on May 11, 2013.

*

Four years later, in 2017, Disney's Pixar releases *Coco*, an animated film that uses Día de los Muertos to normalize the racial contradictions of documentality. Domestically in Trump's America, the movie does poorly. The same year the film is released there is a rise in immigrant deaths on the border. Four hundred and twelve known bodies are recovered. Hundreds are still unfound. In 2018, Disney agrees to a screening of the movie for over four thousand immigrants detained and waiting for their papers on the border. Hundreds will perish in the months that follow. *¡Viva la muerte!*

*

My daughter and I watch the scene in the dark of the theater as light from the screen penetrates my body like an X-ray and reveals a celluloid image of my skeleton. I am not sure if the white faces in the audience are laughing at me or the Mexican Riveras on the screen. I write in the shadows of animation.

Coco, Scene: The Border of the Dead

(Nearby, skeletons exit the Land of the Dead through a gate marked DEPARTURES. Miguel watches.)

DEPARTURES AGENT

Next family, please!

(An ELDERLY COUPLE steps in front of a camera-mounted monitor. The monitor scans their faces and returns an image of their photos on an altar in the Land of the Living.)

DEPARTURES AGENT

Oh, your photos are on your son's *ofrenda*. Have a great visit!

ELDERLY COUPLE

Gracias.

(The couple unites with the rest of their family. They all step onto the bridge, which begins to glow as they gain footing.)

CANNED LOOP

... And remember to return before sunrise. Enjoy your visit!

DEPARTURES AGENT

Next!

(A skeleton man, a smile full of braces, steps up to the monitor.)

DEPARTURES AGENT

Your photo's on your dentist's *ofrenda*. Enjoy your visit!

JUAN ORTODONCIA

Grashiash!

DEPARTURES AGENT

Next!

(HÉCTOR, early twenties, a ragged fellow, steps up to the monitor, disguised as Frida Kahlo.)

HÉCTOR

Yes, it is I. Frida Kahlo.

(beat)

Shall we skip the scanner? I'm on so many *ofrendas*, it'll just overwhelm your blinky thingie . . .

(The monitor scans him, but an "X" appears, accompanied by a negative buzzing sound.)

DEPARTURES AGENT

Well shoot. Looks like no one put up your photo, Frida . . .

(Héctor peels off his unibrow and throws off his frock.)

HÉCTOR

Okay, when I said I was Frida . . . just now? That . . . that was a lie. And
I apologize for doing that.

DEPARTURES AGENT

No photo on an *ofrenda*, no crossing the bridge.

HÉCTOR

You know what, I'm just gonna zip right over, you won't even know
I'm gone.

*(Héctor bolts for the bridge. A security guards blocks the gate. Héctor
splits in two and slides past the guard, half going over, half under.)*

HÉCTOR

Ha Ha!

*(Héctor reaches the bridge at a sprint, but the magic doesn't engage;
he sinks right into the petals.)*

HÉCTOR

Almost there, just a little further . . . !

(The guards saunter to the bridge and casually pull Héctor back toward the Land of the Dead.)

OFFICER

Upsy-daisy . . .

HÉCTOR

Fine, okay. Fine, who cares . . . Dumb flower bridge!

(Miguel watches as the guards haul him out. Tía Rosita looks up in time to see his back.)

TÍA ROSITA

I don't know what I'd do if no one put up my photo.

ARRIVALS AGENT

Next!

TÍA ROSITA

Oh! Come, *mijo*, it's our turn.

(The arrivals line moves forward. The Dead Riveras crowd around the gate. The arrivals agent leans out from his window.)

ARRIVALS AGENT

Welcome back, *amigos*! Anything to declare?

The scene ends: the Riveras are cursed by a short-circuited computer. Cursed or not, my daughter finally sees her name in celluloid and the screen slowly begins to bronze, a perfect hue called "Disney Brown."

*

The effects are revolutionary. Disney has created new techniques to "animate" the dead and create empathy for Mexican skeletons. Animators "spent so much time and research figuring out our human characters and how their skin squashes and stretches, so this totally broke the rules for us. We knew with skeletons that all of a sudden, those boundaries of something organic are gone—the skin, the muscles, the tendons. And if there's nothing holding it together, what can you do with bones? And we realized, we can do all sorts of things." The "thing" is complete: Disney meticulously normalizes the documentality regimes that control life and death on the border, presented perfectly in three dimensions and Dolby THX, trademark pending . . . and a ride at Disneyland awaits approval for construction near Tomorrowland.

MEXICAN MORTALITY PARADOX

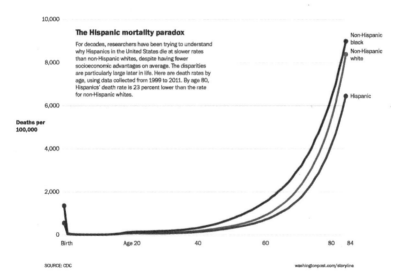

The Hispanic mortality paradox

For decades, researchers have been trying to understand
why Hispanics in the United States die at slower rates
than non-Hispanic whites, despite having fewer
socioeconomic advantages on average. The disparities
are particularly large later in life. Here are death rates by
age, using data collected from 1999 to 2011. By age 80,
Hispanics' death rate is 23 percent lower than the rate
for non-Hispanic whites.

Deaths per 100,000

10,000

8,000

6,000

4,000

2,000

0

Birth · Age 20 · 40 · 60 · 80 · 84

Non-Hispanic black
Non-Hispanic white
Hispanic

SOURCE: CDC

washingtonpost.com/storyline

There is a paradox of the undocumented condition—Mexican and Latinx populations live longer than Anglos and their mortality rate is 25 percent lower, despite the fact that they have worse health care and do not have access to the same services and diets as documented peoples in the United States. Governments have been studying this for decades, seeing what factors have contributed to this phenomenon. One new theory, proposed after testing the blood and saliva of Latinxs, is that their bodies age more slowly than those of other groups, which reveals why they have a slower epigenetic clock. Studies have not concluded how long Latinxs' epigenetic clocks will continue to tick more slowly after they are acculturated into U.S. culture. They keep studying and studying, exploring their undocumented bodies in hopes of finding the fountain of youth.

*

The Mexicans in my family live long lives, despite the mental illness, autoimmune diseases, and heart disease that plague both sides of the family. Pills and surgeries keep us alive well past the life span of average Americans. I was hit with two contributing genetic factors, anxiety and heart disease. I take pills every morning and night to ensure that my heart does not stop, that it stays regulated, and other ones so my mind does not race toward thoughts of my death. And yet, with every pill I take I am reminded of my death, as they remind me of what Stephen Cave calls the mortality paradox, the inevitable and impossible understanding of our actual death. The pills keep me alive and yet, every morning and evening when I swallow them, they point my mind toward my inevitable death. My epigenetic clock is regulated by a pill container that marks my moments with small blue boxes. M.T.W.TH.F.S.SUN. If I stop taking them, I wonder, how long will it take for me to die? I talk to the therapist about this, and he tells me about the two surgeries he is about to have and all of the pills he takes.

"Everyone's body is dying," he tells me; "you need to keep your mind in the present; that will keep you healthy and living longer." His ability to deal with his decaying body does not relieve my existential anxiety. "You know that Mexicans have a higher rate of depression and anxiety than any other group in the U.S.," I tell him. "I did not know that," he says. "Let's breathe together now."

*

My mother calls me and tells me she is no longer going to take aromatase inhibitors to control her hormones, despite the fact that taking these pills will lessen her chances of getting breast cancer again. "They make me crazy, and make me feel like I want to die. If this is living, it is not worth it." I tell her to talk to her doctor and she says the oncologist wants her to take them. "What should I do?" she asks me. I am reminded of my friend who stopped taking AZT because of the horrible side effects and died of AIDS complications a year later. I still miss him and often wonder whether his decision to stop taking the pills led to his death or if it was just his time. I tell my mom I support her decision, knowing that I will lose her one day, but hoping it is not this year. Depression or death is her choice, so she chooses life.

BOOK VIII
Kings and Lords

recollections of ancient things

influenced by some oracle

below the equinoctial line

he was a great **NECROMANCER**

now very visible reveal

indications of its fortune

such until his behavior

Ceased

Governing

Their

Customs

MASCULINITY

N. C. Wyeth. *BILLY THE KID*. 1906. Pen and ink. *The Saturday Evening Post.* Wyeth was commissioned by *The Saturday Evening Post* to do a series of illustrations for Emerson Hough's stories on the West. These illustrations along with Hough's articles provided Americans with more representations of "imitation" bad men.

Billy the Kid (born Henry McCarty, September 17 or November 23, 1859–July 14, 1881, also known as William H. Bonney) was an American Old West outlaw and gunfighter who killed eight men before he was shot and killed at age 21. He took part in New Mexico's Lincoln County War, during which he allegedly took part in three murders.

McCarty was orphaned at age 13. The owner of a boarding house gave him a room in exchange for work. His first arrest was for stealing food at age 16 in late 1875. Ten days later, he robbed a Chinese laundry and was arrested, but he escaped only two days later. He tried to stay with his stepfather, and then fled from New Mexico Territory into neighboring Arizona Territory, making him both an outlaw and a federal fugitive.

After murdering a blacksmith during an altercation in August 1877, Bonney became a wanted man in Arizona Territory and returned to New Mexico, where he joined a group of cattle rustlers. He became a well-known figure in the region when he joined the Regulators and took part in the Lincoln County War. In April 1878, the Regulators killed three men, including Lincoln County Sheriff William J. Brady and one of his deputies. Bonney and two other Regulators were later charged with killing all three men.

Bonney's notoriety grew in December 1880 when the Las Vegas Gazette in Las Vegas, New Mexico, and The Sun in New York City carried stories about his crimes. Sheriff Pat Garrett captured Bonney later that month. In April 1881, Bonney was tried and convicted of the murder of Brady, and was sentenced to hang in May of that year. He escaped from jail on April 28, 1881, killing two sheriff's deputies in the process and evading capture for more than two months. Garrett shot and killed Bonney—aged 21—in Fort Sumner on July 14, 1881. During the following decades, legends that Bonney had survived that night grew, and a number of men claimed to be him.

-WIKIPEDIA-

"Save and Defend us from our ghostly enemies." Scarcely has the news of the killing of William Bonney, alias McCarty, but known the wide-world over as "Billy the Kid," faded from the public mind before we are again to be startled by the second chapter in the bloody romance of his eventual life—the disposal of his body. The stiff was brought to Las Vegas, arriving here at two o'clock in the morning, and was slipped quietly into the private office of a practical "saw-bones," who, by dint of diligent labor and careful watching to prevent detection, boiled and scraped the skin off the "pate" so as to secure the skull. The body, or remains proper, was covered in the dirt in a corral, where it will remain until decomposition shall have robbed the frame of its meat, when the body will be dug up again and the skeleton "fixed-up"—hung together by wires and varnished with shellac to make it presentable.

-*LAS VEGAS OPTIC*, 1881-

For over a century, Mexicans have claimed that Billy the Kid was their father and two Mexican governors have had close associations with him during their political careers. Mexicans refer to him as El Bilito.

-EDITS BY LA MEMORIA TO WIKIPEDIA, OCTOBER 31, 2018, ERASED NOVEMBER 3, 2018-

TODAY

The above facts frame the masculine mythos of Billy the Kid. Lost between Wikipedia entries and official annalists' histories is the reality: Mexican men are haunted by the corpse of Billy the Kid. I am not immune to this appropriation; the specter of Billy the Kid has haunted me for the better part of my life. The haunting didn't begin in 2013, but it is on this date that I find myself driving through the Carrizozo Malpais lava fields, searching for his dead body, his elusive tombstone. I travel through masses of black fissured lava as large as a horse, and I am myself lost in the Valley of Fires. I try to gather my bearings—the map points me toward the east. My journey is a search for Lincoln County, where the last words of Billy the Kid mark the public imagination of the southwestern United States. "*¿Quién es?*"—the last question Billy uttered was one answered with a bullet, and here would begin the public's fascination with a Spanish-speaking Irishman with three mestizo children, and more recently one great-grandson who has been fighting the courts to exhume Billy's body for DNA. I end up in the now-famous hotel where Billy the Kid stayed. Spanish and Western art deco frames a merchandise emporium that sells the legend of Billy the Kid. I am tempted to buy yet another shirt written in Aubrey Landing font: "I am Billy the Kid's Kid." I walk into the room where he slept. I stutter:

"*¿Quién es?*"

Did he dream here? Was his corpse laid on this floor?

Did he write the elusive memoir so many of us have been searching for in the floorboards of these buildings, sold to us as a relic of our Western masculine past?

How does Billy's corpse capture the spectral essence of the masculine Southwest, a space where corpses are exhumed in order to reconstitute the temporal boundaries between the dead and the living in hopes of reifying masculinity?

"¿Quién es?"

✳

YESTERDAY

The kid was disappointed that the mob did not attack the car since it would have unquestionably resulted in his escape. He was on the friendliest terms with the native element of the country; he had protected and helped them in every possible way. . . . In Santa Fe we were allowed to visit the Kid in jail, taking him cigarette papers, tobacco, chewing gum, candy, pies, and nuts. He was very fond of sweets and asked us to bring him all we could.

The kid's general appearance was the same as most boys of his age. I was one month older than Billy. I liked the Kid very much, and long before we even reached Santa Fe, nothing would have pleased me more than to have witnessed his escape. He had his share of good qualities and was very pleasant. He had a reputation for being considerate of the old, the young, and the poor; he was loyal to his friends and above all, loved his mother devotedly. He was unfortunate in starting life and became a victim of circumstance.

In looking back to my first meeting with Billy the Kid, my impressions were most favorable and I can honestly say that he was a "man more sinned against than sinning."

-MIGUEL ANTONIO OTERO, FIRST LATINO TERRITORIAL
GOVERNOR OF NEW MEXICO, *THE REAL BILLY THE KID:
WITH NEW LIGHT ON THE LINCOLN COUNTY WAR*-

We have not put our impressions of him into print. And our silence has been the cause of great injustice to The Kid.

-MARTIN CHAVEZ, QUOTED IN OTERO, *THE REAL BILLY THE KID*-

*

At the turn of the nineteenth century, Miguel Antonio Otero and Teddy Roosevelt met in a brief encounter, though an important one to Otero. The rumor was that Otero was being considered for vice president, or at least a post in Roosevelt's administration. He had already been passed over by McKinley, so perhaps Otero felt this time he would leave New Mexico and enter the White House. His political ambitions would be realized with this meeting. The day Otero met Teddy Roosevelt, Otero wore a traditional Eastern suit and tie, to show that he was as civilized as any other white politician. But beneath his slacks and in his pocket were two hidden objects that would connect him with his Mexican past—the spurs of Billy the Kid and a pocket knife, which had been given to him when the two men met in 1880. This story, as true as all Billy the Kid lore, reveals that Otero's desire was to resurrect Billy the Kid's corpse by wearing a part of him, embodying him through an object, so he could match the masculinity that Roosevelt himself fostered and exploited while he rose as a politician.

To understand Otero's spectral self-fashioning, it is important to point out that he witnessed a period of profound change in masculinity, as it was affected by the expansion and consolidation of the southwestern United States. He was born in 1859, a decade after the Mexican-American War and two years before the Civil War—two wars that would drastically alter the cultural and geographic landscape of America. As his works attest, the most notable changes to occur for Otero would be the closing of the frontier and the annexation of the former Mexican territories as states of the republic. When Otero began his political career in 1893, Frederick Jackson Turner gave his famous "frontier thesis" paper at the American Historical Association's first meeting, held at the World's Columbian Exposition. The paper, titled "The Significance of the Frontier in American History," was a narrative that nicely captured the transition occurring in this period. The frontier experience, he argued, was the defining ethos of American democracy and the American character. After praising America for its imperialist conquest of Native lands and peoples, he concluded his paper with a rather disturbing lament: "Four centuries from the discovery of America, at the end of a hundred of life under the Constitution, the frontier has gone, and with its going has closed the first period of American history." Though he argued this thesis in 1893, Turner's words are rooted in a much more long-standing discourse of white masculinity that began with the signing of the Treaty of Guadalupe Hidalgo in 1848, which ended the Mexican-American War and ceded to the United States millions of acres of Mexican frontier land. At one narrative level, Turner's statements implicitly summarize the imperialist doctrine that America was now in control of the continent from the Atlantic to the Pacific. For Turner to state this boldly meant that Mexican and Native American bodies had now become "part" of the American republic's body politic, but only by means of assimilation, erasure, or dehumanization.

Turner's thesis represents an equally pivotal juncture in Anglo-American/Mexican contact because it also marks an important change that first manifested itself shortly after the Mexican-American War and continued through the late nineteenth century: the realization that America's Manifest Destiny was ending on the continent and that America was entering a period of limited-resource capitalism. Moreover, as Mark Seltzer reminds us, the closing of the frontier consolidated the domination of the nation's topography by the white male body and created a crisis by leaving no more terra incognita to be conquered, which in turn led to heightened public discourses of racism and imperialism in the United States. What was of particular importance for the definition of Anglo-American masculinity and the grounds for its authority was a white male professional-managerial-class annexation of the former Mexican territories, an act presumably ensuring that the Southwest would enter the national body politic as a white member, thus legitimating and maintaining white masculinity as the dominant culture defined it.

The political control of New Mexico, one of the last and economically richest territories of the Southwest, was a particularly enticing prospect for eastern businessmen: its abundant resources, pastoral beauty, and trade routes would garner them millions of dollars. Because New Mexico was mostly Mexican and Native American in population, as well as being politically controlled by bourgeois Nuevomexicanos, the dynamics of Anglo political and economic control were extremely volatile. Indeed, as Miguel Otero recounts in numerous writings both private and public, in the years before Turner's statements, the territory of New Mexico was undergoing profound economic and social changes. What was at stake for bourgeois Nuevomexicanos, Otero would recount, was maintenance of control over the political and public spheres during the transitional period from the old Hispano Nuevo Mexico to the "new" New Mexico.

Otero's peculiar act of writing Billy the Kid's biography, coupled with his "wearing" of Billy, is a moment of inscriptive resurrection, of "ghost writing"; it is a performance of haunting that effectively enabled him to challenge Turner's frontier discourses through Billy's corpse, a rendering of Billy's dead body as a symbolic representation of Mexican barbarism on the frontier. In this way, Otero's rendering of Billy the Kid's biographical corpse creates a prosthesis for Otero's own living body and ironically connects him to a Mexican *gente* he struggled for years to connect with while in New Mexico. Indeed, through

Billy, Otero would foster a political persona wherein he would declare that "[my] blood relations are Mexican" and "[my] ancestors are full-blooded Mexicans."

Otero's participation in the cultural construction of Billy the Kid reveals much about his own masculine desire to foster "Mexican public spirit," as New Mexico's first modern politician would so aptly use in his political speeches. What Otero represents is his own distinctive ability to rise within and, indeed, mimic white masculine discourses of the mass-produced ideas of outlaw manliness, with the result that Billy's body becomes a site for the mediation of Otero's most public cause, New Mexican statehood. We need to remember that at the turn of the last century New Mexicans' bodies were documented as tainted, for they were both "Indian" and "European," and hence constituted in the public sphere as "semicivilized." Therefore, their mestizo bodies were not worthy of being a part of the fraternal brotherhood of the white body politic. Indeed, politicians went so far as to say that New Mexico was far too Mexican and thus should never be a full member of the United States.

Billy the Kid's dead body, which Otero resurrects in his biography, allows Otero to challenge such discourses and resurrect a distinctive Mexican manliness, one that could be documented as part of the United States. It is important to remember that not only for Otero, but also for various dime novelists, and, arguably, for the nation, one of the most publicized characters to represent the dynamic of this period was New Mexico's notorious citizen Billy the Kid. A legend even before his death in 1881, Billy the Kid—personified as both a devil and a saint of the Southwest—would become a mediated corpse through which Euro-Americans and Nuevomexicanos forged a quest for public power in the "new" New Mexico, a colonial endeavor predicated, I want to stress, on competing discourses of American manhood. Like the deaths of Joaquín Murieta in California and Gregorio Cortez in Texas, the death of Billy the Kid, an Irishman named El Bilito in nineteenth-century Mexican corridos, ironically marks an important transition in Anglo-American dominance and colonial contact with Mexicans on the frontier. Implicitly, it is the slaying of the Kid, as well as of these other border hero bodies, that enables Frederick Jackson Turner to argue that the frontier, as a geographical line dividing civilization from savagery, has been closed a little over a decade later.

This colonial document on which Turner's frontier thesis was predicated was represented throughout the literary and political spheres through images of Billy the Kid and later rewritten with Otero's own *The Real Billy the Kid*. In this work, written over the course of his life, Otero transcribes the words of Martin Chavez that I have used as an epigraph above. Chavez was one of the old Nuevomexicano "natives" who rode with Billy the Kid shortly before his death in 1881. After criticizing previous works about Billy the Kid, Chavez tells Otero that Mexican-Americans' impressions of Billy the Kid have not been heard in the public literary sphere; Mexican-Americans have not been able to participate in America's emerging document culture. Chavez's lament is important for a number of reasons, most notably because it shows how the American public is constructed through documentality. Chavez reveals, and Otero enacts through his biography, the fact that print enables them to rewrite the previous stories of Billy the Kid, which characterized the Kid and, by association, Mexicanos in the public imagination as "semicivilized" citizens.

In part, what Otero and, by association, Chavez intend to rewrite through the corpse of Billy the Kid is the "official" discourse within the American literary public spheres, which has associated Billy the Kid's ruthless behavior with Mexican-Americans, as seen especially in the new form of mass publicity that framed discourses about the Kid in the literary public sphere when Otero was a politician: the popular dime novel. The discourse to which Otero responded was first seen throughout the literary sphere of U.S. industrial popular culture in turn-of-the-century dime novels and was continued by Otero's political foes, Pat Garrett and the Santa Fe Ring. In his landmark study *Inventing Billy the Kid*, Stephen Tatum points out that between the years of 1881 and 1906, "dime novels specifically devoted to the Kid's real and imagined exploits were published and sometimes reprinted in New York City, Chicago, St. Louis, and Denver by such houses as Beadle and Adams, Street and Smith, Richard Fox (publisher of the *National Police Gazette*), Frank Tousey, and John W. Morrison."

Most of these dime novels cast Billy the Kid as a barbarian and used racial stereotypes to describe his Mexican surroundings. One of the most popular fiction writers who wrote about the Kid and perpetuated a racist discourse about Mexicanos was Emerson Hough (who used the picture drawn by N. C. Wyeth that begins this chapter), a friend of Pat Garrett and the New Mexican Anglo power structure known as the Santa Fe Ring. In these dime novels, Emerson Hough perpetuated an image of Billy the Kid as a devilish savage and associated the Mexican-American people of New Mexico with his savagery. Therefore, for Hough, the killing of Billy the Kid symbolized the fact that "the Anglo-Saxon civilization was destined to overrun this half-Spanish civilization."

We should note that while Hough's depiction is of a masculine El Bilito, most other dime novelists and fiction writers would characterize Billy the Kid's body as small, racially marked, effeminate, and devilish, which was, coincidentally, the same rhetoric used to characterize Mexican bodies in the Southwest at the turn of the last century. This negative corporeal association was spread throughout the Northeast, for the dime novels about the Kid would sell upward of 150,000 copies, and parts of Hough's works were even published in mass-cultural magazines. Dime novel after dime novel constructed metaphors wherein the Kid's "bloodthirsty" body and "devilish" character were allied with a "border civilization" controlled by corrupt Nuėvomexicanos like Otero.

When considering the haunting power in these fictional treatments, one must not forget what was at stake for Anglo-Saxon manhood during the pivotal decade before Turner would declare the frontier closed and under Anglo-American control. It is no coincidence that while these dime novels were being mass-produced and perpetuating a racialized discourse about Mexicanos, white Anglo-Americans were attempting to consolidate the former Mexican territories into a replica of the white republic. As I mentioned earlier, New Mexico was especially desired for a number of reasons: its mineral resources, trade routes, and pastoral beauty. However, unlike other territories, New Mexico's population was mostly Mexican and Indian, and families like the Oteros had been political scions for generations before the Treaty of Guadalupe Hidalgo.

Reacting to this popular sentiment, Otero addresses the reading public in the preface to *The Real Billy the Kid*, noting that his biography is pure fact and thereby countering those narratives of "pure fiction wholly devoid of fact" that have helped construct the Mexicanos, the Oteros, and the southwestern body politic as uncivilized. Otero's Billy the Kid, by being made a tragic hero who was "more sinned against than sinning" and helped Nuevomexicanos fight against the Santa Fe Ring for Mexican lands, symbolically revealed the injustices that the Mexican-American people had endured after the Treaty of Guadalupe Hidalgo. What Otero's biography explains, then, is how Billy the Kid's body becomes marked in the Mexican community as distinctly Mexican, as El Bilito, a hero of the Mexican-American people. His work was in effect the first call to pardon Billy the Kid, for Billy was, to Otero and other Mexicanos, a "man more sinned against than sinning."

TODAY

The past makes me read slowly, searching for the poetic pardon hidden within the newspaper ink . . .

NO PARDON

"No **Pardon** for the Kid," New Mexico Gov. Bill Richardson **says**. "The romanticism appealed to me . . . but the facts and the evidence did not **support** it."

December 31, 2010, by Rick Rojas, *Los Angeles Times*

Reporting from Phoenix — Despite **a flurry** of publicity and public agonizing, 19th century outlaw Billy the Kid won't be pardoned, outgoing Gov. Bill Richardson announced Friday.

The Democratic governor had considered **pardoning** the Kid since at least the start of **his** term but finally focused on the issue as his term wound down. Friday was the **last** day he could **act**.

"It was **a** very close **call**," Richardson **told** "Good Morning America." "The **romanticism appealed to me**, to issue a pardon, but the facts and the evidence did not support it, and I've got to be responsible, especially when a governor is issuing a pardon."

Richardson considered pardoning the Kid **for one killing**, not **for** any of his **other killings** or crimes. The governor reviewed historical evidence and **a pardon** petition submitted by

Albuquerque lawyer Randi McGinn, but concluded the facts were ambiguous.

McGinn's petition said territorial governor Lew Wallace had promised the Kid a pardon if he testified about a killing he'd witnessed. The Kid, also known as William Bonney and Henry McCarty, offered to testify in return for a pardon in the 1878 slaying of Lincoln County Sheriff William Brady.

Wallace responded: "I have authority to exempt you from prosecution if you will testify to what you say you know."

Bonney testified but received no pardon. Instead, he was convicted and sentenced to hang. In 1881, he broke out of jail, killing two deputies as he fled. Lawman Pat Garrett tracked him down and killed him months later.

The Kid's subsequent conduct factored into his decision, Richardson said Friday.

"What I think maybe tipped the scales with me is that Billy went ahead after not getting this pardon and killed two deputies," he said. He added that "a lack of conclusiveness and the historical ambiguity" also contributed to his decision.

Descendants of Wallace and Garrett had campaigned against the pardon, saying it would have smeared their ancestors' names.

William N. Wallace, great-grandson of the then-governor, expressed relief Friday.

"I was **gratified to** learn that Gov. Richardson had given up his effort to pardon Billy the Kid," Wallace said. "It seems to me he thus followed **a rational**, correct **route**, although I am **still mystified** as to why he commenced this nonsense."

But McGinn found victory in the debate. "We won the battle, which was proving **the broken promise** by Gov. Wallace," she said. "But **we lost** the war."

"It's great being Billy the Kid's lawyer."

Governor Richardson never pardoned Billy the Kid, despite flirting with his corpse for nearly a decade. Like Otero, Richardson used Billy the Kid in his own political self-fashioning. He ordered a special commission to study the case of Billy the Kid, gave him a court-ordered lawyer, and debated the idea of digging up his body to test his DNA and see if he was related to Elbert Garcia. Richardson used the corpse of Billy the Kid as a distraction, a way to connect with the Mexican people he had never truly connected with during his term. His digging up of Billy the Kid enabled him to deflect the political turmoil he had been enduring for over a decade. It is no coincidence that he would connect with his Mexican past and Billy the Kid at the same time that late-night talk shows were using him and his administration to talk about corruption in New Mexican politics and discussing accusations that he used campaign funds to pay off a woman who accused him of sexual harassment. Governor Richardson was a "Mexican Clinton," some would joke, burying the toxic nature of his actions. Even Billy can't help some men's toxic masculinity.

*

Am I as despicable as these men? Have I too used the corpse of Billy the Kid to claim my own Mexicanness, to advance my own career as a Chicanx male in academia? I have worked with Billy the Kid for longer than my daughter has lived. I have presented my arguments to Anglo retirees in their communities; to Western audiences dressed like Wyatt Earp, Pat Garrett, and Billy the Kid, with me in a ten-gallon hat; to academic audiences; to television audiences; and even to Mexicans at a *la raza* conference. Billy—I am allowed to call him by his first name now—has become an institution of the public sphere for me. He has enabled me to get the job I have today.

I am in San Diego with my in-laws. My colleague in Boulder calls me. "PBS's *American Experiences* is looking for you. Everywhere," she says. "You need to call them." Sitting on a park bench in Shelter Island listening to Lyle Lovett practice for his concert at Humphreys, I make a declaration of fact—I tell the producer, "Billy the Kid was a Mexican... No, not a real Mexican, a Mexican like Beck, the singer." Long pause. I don't think he gets it. My entire phone call, my entire contention, centers around a book I recovered while working for the Recovering the U.S. Hispanic Literary Heritage project and which I would later introduce, edit, and partly translate, *The Real Billy the Kid* by Miguel Antonio Otero. The producer googles the book.

"So, Billy the Kid was an honorary Latino?" he asks. Was he then, yesterday, to them? Now, to me? "Perhaps," I say.

"What are you saying, then?"

I interrupt, "OK, he is to me. Billy the Kid was as Mexican as I am Mexican."

Long pause.

He wanted a black-and-white answer to a brown question. Billy's phantom documentality, his ability to be anything to anyone, his ability to take on so many truths, so much history and memory, allowed for Latinos to use him—no, strike that, to embody him.

"So is there a real Billy the Kid?" he continues the conversation.

"No, no more than there is a real George Washington."

Long pause.

"I'll get back to you," he says.

I sense his skepticism. I retrace my steps back to Lyle Lovett. I stand on the other side of the marina. I can barely make him out onstage. He is wearing a bolo tie and a hat. I wish I could tell you he was singing his song "Me and Billy the Kid." Wait, I will tell you that. While I had the conversation with the producer, Lyle Lovett was singing "Me and Billy the Kid." It was memorable.

I wanted to tell him I began working on Billy the Kid in the middle of what I call my Chicano years. The years in graduate school when I reread all Latino history, searching for a Chicano everywhere. Elvis, not El Vez, I swore was Chicano. Martin Sheen, his kids: yeah, Latinos. Even today, I secretly search for Chicanos. I search in vain for Chicanos in the public sphere in order to locate my own identity. I think I am a Chicano because I know they are out there. Why else would I search for them in the present and in the past? Miguel Antonio Otero (1859–1944) stood as my first interlocutor with Billy the Kid. My first exploration of "Mexicanness." As I have talked about above, like me, he, too, would use the Kid to fashion his own Latino identity. And like him, I would write a book about Billy the Kid in order to fashion my own masculinity within the academy.

But I am not alone. Other Mexican scholars and writers would resurrect Billy the Kid for their own reasons, but all to hide and prop up their own toxic masculinity. No less than the first winner of the Premio Quinto Sol, Rudolfo Anaya, would also resurrect Billy the Kid . . .

Theatre & plays

La Casa Teatro
133 E. Hwy. 66, Apt. #3 - Albuquerque, NM 87123
tele. (505) 275-0716

PRESS RELEASE

WORLD PREMIER PERFORMANCE

LA CASA TEATRO presents a bilingual play, _Billy The Kid_, written by Rudolfo Anaya and directed by Cecilia Aragón. The world premiere of _Billy The Kid_ will be presented at the South Broadway Cultural Center in July.

This play depicts the life of Billy the Kid and his impact on New Mexico's culturally diverse history. *El Bilito's* story is narrated by two characters, Mr. Ashley and Don Paco who were directly involved in his life. Each tells his point of view which leads to flashbacks of his unlawful activities, his involvement with Hispano familias and the Anglo community and ultimately his untimely death.

Billy The Kid will be playing at the South Broadway Cultural Center. Evening performances will be July 11th, 12th, 18th, and 19th at 8:00 p.m., and Sunday Matinees on July 13th and 20th at 2:00 p.m. General Admission is $8.00, students and senior citizens $5.00.

Rudolfo Anaya (playwright) and his family will be our honored guests at the GALA reception on Saturday July 12th at 7:00 p.m. (open to the public).

If you are interested in helping us sponsor this event or need further information call (505) 275-0716.

ACT 1

The men pull Paco away. They cover Billy with a sheet, then slowly raise the bed and carry it out as if carrying a coffin. Rosa follows, the other women comforting her. Paco remains. Ash rises from his stool and looks at the audience. The actors sing "El Corrido de Billy the Kid."

Fue una noche oscura y triste
En el pueblo Fort Sumner
Cuando el sheriff Pat Garrett
A Billy the Kid mató
A Billy the Kid mató

Mil ochocientos ochenta y uno
Presente lo tengo yo
Cuando en la casa de Pedro Maxwell
Nomás dos tiros le dio
Nomás dos tiros le dio

Vuela, vuela palomita,
A los pueblos de Río Pecos
Cuéntale a las morenitas
Que ya su Billy murió
Que ya su Billy murió

Ay, qué tristeza me da
Ver a Rosita llorando,
Y el pobre Billy en sus brazos
Con su sangre derramando
Con su sangre derramando

Vuela, vuela palomita,
A los pueblos de Río Pecos

Cuéntale a las morenitas
Que ya su Billy murió

ASH: You Mexicans. Yes, you had a soft spot in your heart for Billy. He spoke Spanish like a native . . .

PACO: He treated us like hombres! Mexicano or gringo, todos éramos iguales.

I stalk Anaya, write him countless letters asking him why it is he decided to write about Billy the Kid, to spend so much time with this Irish white boy. He responds to me in a letter, telling me Billy was an important figure for New Mexicans and he wanted to capture the man who has been so misunderstood for generations.

*

I read and reread Anaya's letter weeks before I begin my journey through the lava fields, this New Mexican Valley of Fires, lost, searching again for Billy the Kid's grave in every fissure. I hum the corrido "El Bilito" and drive parallel to the train rails that have not been used in decades. I wonder if my great-grandfather, Manuel Pérez, who drove the train of the exiled Pancho Villa, ever made it down this far. The search for Billy leads me to my nostalgic search for masculinity and rebellion in my own family, an ancestral link to a Mexican Revolutionary past that is so distant from the life we all have made for ourselves—we now are a family of academics. I have never even been on a train. So I am left searching for the public grave of Billy the Kid, a white Irish immigrant, uncovering his Mexican past with every news story. I still search, of course, but now through my rearview mirror. I am not sure what the truth is anymore. Was Billy the Kid Mexican? Was my great-grandfather really a conductor, or did he tell us a story about the revolution and trains that somehow over the years turned him into a bandit's accomplice? I plan on sending out my DNA, someday. I finally find Billy's tomb—a plaque ends my search, pointing me to a stone relic marking the remains of William Henry McCarty, Jr. Born 1859. Died 1881. I am underwhelmed. Two weeks after my visit to the stone in Fort Sumner, New Mexico, a group of vandals attempt to steal it. The two thousand pounds of unbearable weight is too much for the vandals, however. They are not "man enough" to carry the weight, I suspect. They only manage to make off with the plaque that marks the way to his remains. Now an iron cage shaped like a jail surrounds the tombstone. Billy's corpse is finally entombed. But his ghost has long ago escaped.

RESURRECTION

Los Angeles Times

LARGEST CIRCULATION IN THE WEST, 992,875 DAILY, 1,317,220 SUNDAY.

FINAL
ONE OF THE WORLD'S
GREAT NEWSPAPERS

VOL. LXXXIX +1   SIXTEEN SECTIONS—SECTION A   CC   SUNDAY, AUGUST 30, 1970   586 PAGES   Copyright © 1970 Los Angeles Times   SUNDAY 50c

DISPERSAL—Sheriff's Department officers charge across Laguna Park field to break up crowd of demonstrators gathered in the open area.
Times photo by Eric Bronx

Ruben Salazar
Times staff

One Dead, 40 Hurt in East L.A. Riot

Times Columnist Ruben Salazar Killed by Bullet

BY CHARLES T. POWERS
and JEFF PERLMAN
Times Staff Writers

An East Los Angeles parade and rally that attracted about 20,000 persons to demonstrate Mexican-American opposition to the war in Southeast Asia erupted into a riot Saturday, claiming the life of one of the city's leading spokesmen for Chicano rights.

The dead man was Ruben Salazar, 42, award-winning Times columnist and news director for television station KMEX (Channel 34).

Deputies found him sprawled on the floor inside the Silver Dollar

Eyewitness story, details of Salazar's death, more pictures on Page B.

Cafe, 4945 Whittier Blvd., with a bullet wound in the head.

The officers had surrounded the bar and ordered it evacuated after receiving a report of a man carrying a gun inside.

Tear gas—but no bullets—was fired inside, deputies said, and two men, a woman and a child left the building through a back door. One of the men, deputies said, was carrying a gun.

At 5:30 p.m., nearly two hours later, deputies in the area were approached by a man who said, "I think there's somebody in the bar." It was Mr. Salazar.

The bar had been near the center of a storm of rioting that swept through the neighborhood along Whittier Blvd., leaving more than 40 persons injured—one of them apparently near death.

At the peak of the turmoil, a dozen fires burned out of control along

Whittier Blvd., the main axis of the disturbance, as about 500 police and sheriff's deputies teamed with riot equipment near Whittier and Atlantic Blvds.

Windows were smashed in virtually every store along a 12-block strip of Whittier Blvd., and looting was heavy, deputies reported.

By midnight, the East Los Angeles Sheriff's substation had reported 103 arrests, including 25 who were arrested as they rode down Olympic Blvd. in a truck reportedly carrying ammunition and three rifles, all said to have been recently fired.

County Fire Department officials said firemen were being shot at and were ducking barrages of rocks and bottles as they attempted to get to the largest of the fires along Whittier Blvd.

Throughout a three-square-mile area—bounded roughly by Indiana St. on the west, Atlantic Blvd. on the east, the Pomona Freeway on the north and Olympic Blvd. on the south—there were repeated clashes

Please Turn to Page 18, Col. 1

DANCING GIRLS, CAMEL MILK

Araby Sheiks Shake Off Dust of Desert in Lebanon Oasis

BY WILLIAM TUOHY
Times Staff Writer

ALEY, Lebanon—The Cadillacs and Mercedes inch along bumper-to-bumper on the main street, a desert sheik will occasionally butcher a sheep in the bathtub of his resort hotel, and the nightclubs pay hoodlum protection money in the best U.S. gangland tradition.

This is Aley, the summer resort capital of the Middle East, where the wealthier Arabs flee the furnace-like heat of the Arabian Peninsula and sample the unaccustomed fleshpots, nonexistent in their conservative Moslem countries.

Here, far removed from the Arab-

Israeli conflict and the peace talks, the visitors escape the 125-degree heat of the lowlands and desert, and relax in the cool breezes 800 feet in the Lebanese mountains.

Lebanese government officials, too, used to take up residence here each summer, until the incoming, free-spending sheiks drove the prices out of reach.

A villa with three floors, eight bedrooms, sitting rooms, servant rooms, and two dining rooms would run about $7,000 for the three-month season. Smaller villas would be correspondingly lower.

PANEL ON CAMPUS UNREST TO STUDY MADISON BOMBING

BY THOMAS J. FOLEY
Times Staff Writer

WASHINGTON—President Nixon's Commission on Campus Unrest Saturday ordered a staff investigation of the bombing of the University of Wisconsin mathematics study center.

Commission staff director Matt Byrne Jr., former U.S. attorney in Los Angeles, said the decision was reached at an executive session meeting Saturday morning in Washington. He indicated the information obtained would be used to help the commission in the preparation of its report on violence on American campuses.

The bombing Monday caused an estimated $6 million in damage, took the life of a mathematics researcher

Hashish-Smuggling U.S. Plane Seized on Island of Crete

IRAKLION, Crete (UPI)—A U.S. twin-engine plane carrying $570,000 worth of smuggled hashish was seized on this Greek island Saturday after being chased across the Mediterranean by Lebanese and Greek jet fighters.

Police said five Americans aboard the Convair 240 were arrested. The plane and its cargo of 1,467 pounds of hashish were seized.

Before the jets forced them to land at Iraklion airport, the men had swapped cigarets for hashish at a Lebanese landing strip and made off through a hail of police gunfire, officials in Beirut reported.

THE ... MURDER ... AND RESURRECTION OF RUBEN SALAZAR BY THE LOS ANGELES COUNTY SHERIFF'S DEPARTMENT ... SAVAGE POLARIZA-TION & THE MAKING OF A MARTYR ... BAD NEWS FOR THE MEXICAN-AMERICAN ... WORSE NEWS FOR THE PIG ... AND NOW THE NEW CHI-CANO ... RIDING A GRIM NEW WAVE ... THE RISE OF THE BATOS LOCOS ... BROWN POWER AND A FISTFUL OF REDS ... RUDE POLITICS IN THE BAR-RIO ... WHICH SIDE ARE YOU ON ... BROTHER? ... THERE IS NO MORE MIDDLEGROUND ... NO PLACE TO HIDE ON WHITTIER BOULEVARD ... NO REFUGE FROM THE HELICOPTERS ... NO HOPE IN THE COURTS ... NO PEACE WITH THE MAN ... NO LEVERAGE ANYWHERE ... AND NO LIGHT AT THE END OF THIS TUNNEL ... NADA ...

-HUNTER S. THOMPSON, "STRANGE RUMBLINGS IN AZTLAN,"
ROLLING STONE, 1971-

A stamp's act of commemorating the dead lends itself to a mass-produced official resurrection of the body like no other document in U.S. culture. The USPS resurrected Ruben Salazar in 2008 as part of a series of stamps that honored American journalists. Salazar's stamp would, at the time, be only the second in U.S. history to document a Mexican-American, the first being César Chávez. When the Ruben Salazar stamp was issued in 2008, I had long since ended my stamp collecting obsession. I began collecting the same year I got my first volume of the *World Book Encyclopedia*. The encyclopedia collection came with a set of stamps from twenty-five cities around the world. For five dollars a month, I could get an additional hundred stamps. That I was introduced to philately through my first encyclopedia is ironic. Today, printed stamps, like encyclopedias, are undergoing a slow death: both relegated to the category of dead documents, their useful value having passed; both lost in libraries, grocery store registers, and boxes in attics. Salazar's stamp still hangs on my wall, a 22K gold–plated hologram bound in glass, a proof waiting for a printing press that no longer exists. Three years after Salazar's stamp was issued, in 2011, his case was reopened and investigated by the Los Angeles County Office of Independent Review. A twenty-page report reviewed all of the historical documents to ascertain whether or not he had been murdered. The document's conclusions were inconclusive, but at least we have a stamp of his image, a 42-cent martyr.

*

Review of the Los Angeles County Sheriff's Department's Investigation into the Homicide of Ruben Salazar

A Special Report by the
Los Angeles County Office of Independent Review
February 22, 2011

Conclusion:

Ruben Salazar was a powerful advocate for the Latino community who became an icon for journalists and for those advancing the cause of civil rights through exposure of injustices. His untimely and tragic death by means of a tear gas projectile fired by a sheriff's deputy led to a diminishment of trust between some in the Latino community and the sheriff's department. We have detailed in the report how the lack of transparency by the sheriff's department in 1970 and a number of questions left unanswered by the homicide investigation continue to cause some to challenge the official results and question why those involved were never prosecuted for their roles in Mr. Salazar's death. To the degree the eight boxes of documents retained by the Homicide Bureau shed additional light on Mr. Salazar's death forty years ago, this report is intended to provide a narrative to those materials. However, the insight provided by these documents is lacking in that the homicide investigation did not attempt to directly address the questions that linger—namely, the suspicion by some that Mr. Salazar was targeted that day by law enforcement. Moreover, because the scope of the department's investigation and subsequent inquest was limited to reviewing whether a crime had been committed, a more exacting review of the tactical flaws, poor decision making, and other potential performance deficiencies did not occur. With those limitations, we are hopeful that this account of the materials that do exist will provide a fuller account of the events that day . . . an account that is long overdue.

BOOK IX
Merchants

History

             speaks of supernatural

phenomena

                                    where

generations of people

dwell

as a thing

contrary to human nature

PURGATORY (MICTLĀN)

You have brought yourself to the place of mystery, the place of the unfleshed, the place where there is arriving, the place with no smoke hole, the place with no fireplace. No longer will you make your way back, your return. No more will you consider your present, your past. For a little while you have gone leaving orphans, you have gone leaving people, your children, your grandchildren . . .

-FLORENTINE CODEX-

✳

* In the United States, there are as many as 80,000 detainees in custody.
* Thousands go missing every year, never to be seen again.
* In 2015, ICE requests to destroy documents pertaining to detainees and their deaths.
* In 2017, 1,500 detained children go missing. No records can be found.
* In 2018, transgender detainees are not given equal rights and are murdered at a higher rate than any other detained group. No records can be found of hundreds of these victims, nor can they be located.
* 4,500 undocumented youth are sexually assaulted from 2015 to 2018.
* Private companies are making billions by holding detainees. The Trump administration refuses to release exact numbers and the processes for awarding contracts. A *Daily Beast* report finds that in 2018 alone one billion dollars were spent on private facilities to hold undocumented people.
* On March 19, 2019, the Supreme Court rules 5–4 in *Nielsen v. Preap* that detainees can be incarcerated indefinitely. Purgatory is now a legal space for Latinxs living in the United States.

SANCTUARY

*Sanctuary is a word derived from the Latin **sanctuarium**, which is, like most words ending in **-arium**, a container for keeping something in—in this case holy things or perhaps cherished people (**sanctae/sancti**). The meaning was extended to places of holiness or safety, in particular the whole demarcated area, often many acres, surrounding a Greek or Roman temple; the original terms for these are **temenos** in Greek and **fanum** in Latin, but both may be translated as "sanctuary." Similar usage may be sometimes found describing sacred areas in other religions. In Christian churches **sanctuary** has a specific meaning, covering part of the interior, covered below.*

-WIKIPEDIA-

There's a big change of heart, of mind, of people don't want sanctuary cities. They're dangerous; they don't want them anymore. . . . You wouldn't believe how bad these people are. These aren't people. These are animals.

-PRESIDENT DONALD TRUMP, CALIFORNIA SANCTUARY STATE
ROUNDTABLE, MAY 16, 2018-

There are thousands of sanctuary cities and spaces throughout the United States, spaces that defy the policies of the Trump administration and provide a safe harbor for those persecuted in both their native countries and the United States. These people are subjects in between countries, in between documents of belonging, and so they live in limbo, lost in a bureaucratic system that relegates their lives to small rooms in churches and temples across the United States. I found purgatory in a room off the front hall of Temple Micah in Denver, Colorado, in a designated sanctuary, where the undocumented woman Araceli Velásquez and her U.S.-born children currently reside. I call attention to this particular "sanctuary" because in May of 2018, the same period when Trump had his forum on sanctuary cities, I found myself in this sanctuary, not searching for relief but rather visiting the temple for a friend's son's bar mitzvah. Between the ceremonies, I found myself searching the halls of the temple and came across Velásquez's sanctuary. The door was open and I saw her sitting on her bed in a two-hundred-square-foot room. Alone. Her children were not there. She looked at me and smiled. I was embarrassed, felt as if I was intruding on her life. I apologized, *"Lo siento." "¿Para qué?"* she said. We smiled and I walked away, ashamed of gazing upon her life. I asked myself on the way home, "If this is sanctuary, what is safety? What is happiness?"

In the days following I find out that Araceli Velásquez has become a symbol in our mass document culture for people held in sanctuaries across the country. Congressional representative Diana DeGette visited her and, standing hand in hand with her, argued that we need immigration reform. But what happens when the cameras stop intruding, when my eyes are no longer gazing upon her life? Velásquez and her family are left alone in sanctuary, where their lives have been dramatically altered, living in indefinite limbo as if in detention; the days become weeks and the weeks months and the months years. As with indefinite detainees across the country, Ms. Velásquez, I find out, has not been able to leave her room for over a year, her health having deteriorated dramatically in that time. She feels like she is under constant stress with no outlet for exercise. Consequently, she says, "I have gained a lot of weight." Because there are no windows or natural light, "vision has deteriorated." She says that she has constant headaches, her eyes tear, she fights dizziness. *Sanctuary* for her "is a physical and mental struggle," which she laments has led to depression, as "she is dying of sadness." In the end, her depressive symptoms are similar to those of thousands who are detained across the country: millions of undocumented dying of sadness somewhere lost in sanctuary.

Weeks later I ask my friend about volunteering, bringing food or standing watch against ICE. I find out there are so many volunteers that there is a waiting list. Everyone wants to help the undocumented in designated sanctuary spaces. I contemplate interviewing her for this book. What can I ask that has not been asked already? Should I ask her what it's like to live in a temple? Is she being treated well? How would she characterize her quality of life? Is she happy? I realize that doing so would be no different than that moment when I intruded upon her life, staring in at her home, at her sanctuary. As hospitable as the thousands of people and spaces associated with the sanctuary movement across the United States are, I cannot stop wondering—are these spaces really sanctuaries? Do we really want the undocumented to leave these safe spaces? Do we all gaze upon their pain in these spiritual places of worship to remind us of our happiness, our pain? Whose sanctuary is it after all? I, we, cannot forget that I write, you read, this entry while she remains in purgatory, dying of sadness.

POSSESSION

Everyone wants to possess the undocumented for profit, to inhabit the skin of their dead bodies as if it were a fashion accessory gilded with guilt upon our living bodies.

In 2014, a reality show is produced to highlight six "average" Americans who are confronted with the realities of immigration while retracing the footsteps of dead border runners. The first episode shows them going to the morgue to pick out the corpse they will be assigned to follow. They rummage through their belongings and documents and the host proclaims, "We've given them a name. You must give them a story," and an undocumented Amazing Race ensues over the course of six episodes that play on Al Jazeera at midnight.

The same year, the video game *The Migrant Trail* is released. Styled after the iconic *Oregon Trail*, it allows you to either "play as a migrant" or play as "a border patrol." In 2016, the popular game *Cruis'n USA* creates a race car simulator on which you play as a migrant who has recently entered the United States and tries to find food and documents, all while speeding through the highways of L.A.

In 2017, Alejandro González Iñárritu writes, directs, and produces the VR film *Carne y arena* (*Flesh and Sand*) and presents it at the Cannes Film Festival. The film places the viewer among a group of immigrants who are led by a coyote across the Mexican border into the United States until they are stopped by the border patrol. According to Iñárritu, "No experience in Carne y Arena will never be the same for any visitor. We created a truthful alternate space where you as a visitor will walk alongside the immigrants (and into their minds) with infinite possibilities and perspectives within a vast landscape, but you will go on your own terms." It is hailed by critics as a new form of immersion that will take film to new levels of "experience," as "the result is an extraordinary verisimilitude, an amazing experience of moving through a virtual world. . . . This takes us back to the early days of cinema, before the Lumière brothers invented public screenings with projectors. VR is very much like the Edison Kinetoscopes in the Nickelodeon parlors in the early 1900s." You are, as the subtitle of the film suggests, "virtually present, physically invisible"—this subtitle describes how VR changes the nature of the audience; it plunges "viewers into the harsh life of an immigrant," and in this way "a fusion of identities arises: a psychophysical unity in which, by crossing the threshold of the virtual, the human strays into the imaginary and vice versa. It is a revolution in communication in which seeing is transformed into feeling and into a physical engagement with cinema: a transition from the screen to the gaze of the human being, with a total immersion of the senses."

The same year, in Boulder, I sign up to take the one-hour "immersive" tour called Forced from Home, which is sponsored by Doctors Without Borders. Complete with virtual reality videos, props, and 360-degree perspectives on the lives of undocumented immigrants and migrants, the experience shows us what it is like to live and feel as a migrant. We see what they carry, how they live in detention and migrant centers, what they eat, and how they cope with the harsh realities of living undocumented day to day. I take the one-hour tour with the predominately white students in my Latinx studies class, an extra-credit assignment. Three students attend. We go to Starbucks after the tour to talk about what we felt, what we experienced. I sit and listen to my students talk about the pain they felt. "It was so real," one says. "I feel so bad for them," another chimes in. I smile and understand their guilt and continue to sip my espresso as I look at the long line of white Boulderites standing to get into the exhibit situated in the middle of Pearl Street. "I feel it too," I say.

BOOK X
The People

I follow the order of persons—

Of the body

Of eternal and external organs

Of the ailments

Of learning and practicing

Of astrology

Of theology

Of our Catholic Faith

Of their habits

Of this land

Of the state

Of our dwellings

Of idolatry and drunkenness

Of time and unbelief

Of language

Of mind

Of grammar

AZTEC CHILDREN
(MÁXIMO Y BARTOLA)

Aztec (Az·tec): **1A**: a member of the Nahuatl-speaking people that founded the Mexican empire conquered by Cortés in 1519. **B**: a member of any people under the Aztec influence.

Child, *plural* **Children** (Chil·dren): **1A**: a young person especially between infancy and puberty.

Aztec Children: **1A**: a documented curiosity.

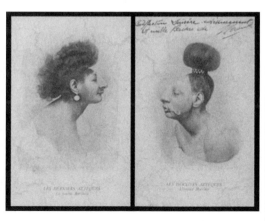

Máximo and Bartola were born microcephalic. They were originally from a village near Usulután in El Salvador and entered history in 1848, the year the U.S.-Mexico War ended and thousands of miles of Mexican lands were ceded to the United States. There are two stories of their existence. The first is taken from a thirty-five-page document published in 1850, *Memoir of an Eventful Expedition in Central America: Resulting in the Discovery of the Idolatrous City of Iximaya in an Unexplored Region and the Possession of Two Remarkable Aztec Children, Descendants and Specimens of the Sacerdotal Caste (Now Nearly Extinct) of the Ancient Aztec Founders of the Ruined Temples of That Country.* In it, Pedro Velasquez recounts the travels to terra incognita, the Aztec lands in Mexico, where he "finds" the last two Aztecs alive, Máximo and Bartola. The second story, recounted in some encyclopedias, follows the travels of Ramón Selva, a Spanish trader who, while in a village in El Salvador, found the two teenage children and saw money in their curious disposition. After negotiating with their family, he promised to bring them to America and cure their microcephaly. Máximo and Bartola never returned to El Salvador. Instead they were exhibited throughout the world as curiosities: as the last Aztecs to breathe. As relics of a lost civilization, Máximo and Bartola toured with P. T. Barnum for decades, renamed "the Aztec Wonders." During and after their lifetime, their base material existence helped promote phrenology and other pseudoscientific systems of belief, as well as aesthetic currents like surrealism.

*

They were considered Barbarians, as a people at the lowest level of perfection, when in reality (excluding some injustices their mode of government contained) in matters of good conduct they surpass many other nations which have great confidence in their administration.... It is certainly a matter of great wonderment that, for so many centuries, our Lord has concealed a forest of so many idolatrous people whose luxuriant fruits only the demon harvested and holds hoarded in the eternal fire.

-BERNARDINO DE SAHAGÚN, *FLORENTINE CODEX*, 1675-

No words can describe my astonishment, at the very first glimpse I caught of these little beings of our race in "miniature," Aztec Children, pigmies of the smallest size yet every limb and part of the body, from the crown of the head to the sole of the foot, in the most perfect harmony and proportion. No deformity—no perturbance—no diminution of one part of the body at the expense of another, as is seen in dwarfs—no wrinkled, parchment skin—no sign of premature decay, but the whole body free from spot or blemish, and the whole figure in the most perfectly agreeable proportion.

-WASHINGTON IRVING, *ENCYCLOPEDIA OF IRVING*, 1853,
QUOTED IN PEDRO VELASQUEZ, *MEMOIR OF AN
EVENTFUL EXPEDITION* . . . -

White men and women have, as we know, tenaciously persisted in their efforts to regain at last, a human face ... so many strange, merely half-monstrous individuals seem to persist in empty animation, like the jingle of the music box, innocent vice, libidinous heat, lyrical fumes.

-GEORGES BATAILLE, DOCUMENTS, "AZTEC SACRIFICE,"
DATE UNKNOWN-

I am an Aztec Angel
criminal
of a scholarly
society
I do favors
for whimsical
magicians
Where I pawn
my heart
for truth
and find
my way
through obscure
streets
of soft spoken
Harakiris.

-LUIS OMAR SALINAS, "AZTEC ANGEL," 1971-

*

Negative Automation: Bataille's base material, the new Victorian gentleman and woman, merely half-monstrous individuals, a couple on wet plate photo, glass tinged, 27 mm high, 20 mm wide, gold-colored brass matt, framed black, silver nitrate coated with collodion, sepia subject—Aztec Children—frame long, standing, dark skin, dark clothes, wrinkled, half-Victorian, half-monstrous, figures remain still, hunched over, him, hair black, teased perfectly, her, four feet tall, head small, nose large, human figure on Jefferson Ave., Detroit, Michigan.

373, 373, 373, 373, three hundred and seventy-four pictures. What an ugly specimen I have become, a man with a beard. I stare at the mirror before each frame, teasing my hair, teasing Bartola's hair with this old comb, flakes off the metal forks tear at her skin. She never complains. We no longer look at each other anymore. I see her only in glimpses, reflections of who we were and now are, to perfect the look of the other takes time, takes money, takes imagination. What she has become in my mind is what she has become in yours now. She was and is so beautiful, like me, under this glass. I stare at the mirror one last time. The real Aztec I have become in your own image of imagination, a people I never knew, never felt. A book once told me who I was, a real scientist classified me as Aztec, a memory of conquest. Who are we now? I never think this anymore.

373, 373, 373, 373, three hundred and seventy-four pictures. What an ugly specimen I have become, a woman with a beard. I no longer stare at the mirror before each frame. Máximo teases my hair, delicate strokes from a pick tinged with rust help the hair lift. I wonder if Máximo remembers what I once looked like, who I once was before these clothes. I no longer remember before these clothes. Him or me. They give us reports and news clippings. I no longer read them. They frame me sitting always. Sitting beneath a man I once knew. Standing now. When this ends will I still be me or will I be the picture? We are now scattered throughout the world, silver nitrate exposures on glass, sepia refracting my thoughts through wet chemical images. I cannot find one exposure.

*

Máximo and Bartola both died around the year 1890. Their graves unmarked and unknown, only documents remain. Their images haunt me.

Ancestors/objects outside of myself led me to these documents, to archives foundational, to hypervisible people rendered invisible in cages. I have been able to stand back from afar, look at my own otherness through objects made inanimate in my mind . . . my touch grows cold with every document I read to frame my evidence, my criteria of their existence, nonessential to a fault. Like a doctor upon the body, my documents of another people spark a curiosity of self, of others who seem to look like me but never seem to be me, to see me, never reaching an origin of my species. When will I see and feel like them? When will I know where my story begins? I continue to search; curiosity motivates my gaze upon others who talk in another tongue, who consume another life. I study the motivation of Others who want to disappear into an originary skin. I disappear behind documents. I objectify. I worry: Have I become accursed by Bataille's pineal eye? Do I gaze upon my own people?

PHANTOM LIMBS

Apotheosis of a Leg: *Reports of death alternated with those of Santa Anna's miraculous recovery until it was finally ascertained that the surgeons had successfully removed his badly mangled leg below the knee. As the patient convalesced, the leg was buried in the grounds of the hacienda and pious deputations from the capital deposited wreaths on this grave. His leg doubtless handicapped him ... but its disabilities were more cerebral than physical.*

*

*The ornate funeral ceremonies that General Santa Anna ordered to be per-
formed in 1842 for his leg, which was lost while fighting the French at the Battle
of Veracruz in 1838, are often seen as the culmination of that caudillo's vain-
glory and megalomania. After being amputated, the leg spent four years buried
at Santa Anna's hacienda, Manga de Clavo, in Veracruz. When Santa Anna
resumed the presidency in late 1841, he had the limb dug up, placed in a crystal
vase, and taken amid a full military dress parade to Mexico City (escorted by
the presidential bodyguard, the army, and cadets from the military academy),
where it was buried beneath an elaborate monument. The funeral involved
cannon salvos, speeches, and poems in the general's honor, and it was attended
by the entire cabinet, the diplomatic corps, and the Congress.*

*

*Why should anyone criticize if a funeral is performed for the foot, arm, or hair
of an illustrious general?*

*Passions always tarnish merit with malevolence and really do not wish true merit
celebrated. So answer quickly and with confidence: Why should we not honor merit
in the lifeless limb of a great and heroic caudillo? Why should anyone criticize?*

*To make this fitting obloquy to a sacrificed limb—not to the man, but to what he
has given fearlessly for the Fatherland—it would be unjust, ungrateful, foolish,
and disloyal to claim it is not lawful or right that a lone foot have a tomb or
mausoleum, that a funeral be performed.*

*Did Artemisia not hide the ashes of Mausolus in her breast and believe this the
only remedy? She did her duty. So today Mexico erects a tomb reaching to the
sky, covering with ardent hope a jewel of History, and giving glory to the foot,
arm, or hair.*

There is a maxim which states a cherished principle: If one kisses the hem of a robe it is because of the Saint who wears it; thus, it is not for the foot itself; on the contrary, though traitors may complain that we say, for good or ill, "Viva!" be assured that the people are grateful to an illustrious general.

✻

Nothing in life is permanent, God alone remains, so the things of this world are here today and gone tomorrow.

If we search through all of history we will not find a single soul whose triumphs and glory last for all eternity. Even so, our memory of great heroes is eternal; though no one can be constant in their conduct or their lives, for until death arrives, nothing in life is permanent.

Such may be said of Santa Anna's foot, which was placed in Santa Paula [Cemetery] with such solemn pomp and majesty; and today the Mexican populace, after rising in rebellion, full of enthusiasm and zeal, took the foot from the sepulchre; so it is clear that on the earth God alone remains.

At that hour and moment the foot's owner was far away; but around here his FOOT was walking around with the rebels. It is certain that no one felt any pain from this; but I believe that such an unthinkable act could only have been done by the things of this world.

At other times this foot was earnestly respected; but that was when its owner still held us in subjugation; today the people have treated it like a dirty old bone, because the nation no longer wishes to stand for it; because, in the end, good and evil are here today and gone tomorrow.

-ANONYMOUS, 184?-

*

Stop! I don't wish to hear any more! Almighty God! A member of my body, lost in the service of my country, dragged from the funeral urn, broken into bits to be made sport of in such a barbaric manner!

-ANTONIO LÓPEZ DE SANTA ANNA, *THE EAGLE*, 1844-

*

What happens when part of your body becomes a ghost, a specter that chews on nerves that only your mind can see and feel? Explaining phantom limb pain is like documenting a ghost with a camera. There is never enough light, the image always blurred, so everyone doubts your vision. Phantom limbs dwell in my father's father, Narciso "Shorty" Rivera, who had his thumb amputated when he was a young man. Some say a rice mill accident caused an infection that turned to gangrene in 1947, and they had to cut his thumb off so the gangrene would not spread. He never told us exactly how it happened, only that it hurt for years after it was gone. "Do you miss having a thumb?" I would ask him. "Only when it hurts," he would say with a smile. Exactly one hundred years before my grandfather lost his thumb, General Santa Anna lost his prosthetic leg during the U.S.-Mexico War in 1847, the year before the Treaty of Guadalupe Hidalgo was inscribed and would cut the body politic of Mexico into pieces, creating phantom limbs for millions of Mexicans for generations. I wonder if Santa Anna still feels the pain of losing his leg, of losing the war. Millions of undocumented Mexicans still feel the pain in their prosthetic bodies.

BODY

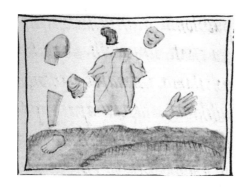

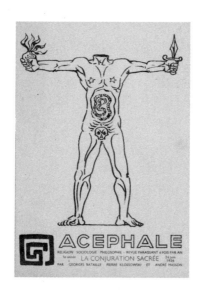

*

~Skin~

Our skin

Our outer skin

White

Ruddy

Chili-red

Very chili-red

Very ruddy swarthy

Swarthy

Swarthy

Dirty-colored

Black

Black

Black

Rubber-colored

Chalky

Ashen

Warm

Cold

Cold

Cold

Very cold

Very cold

Cold

Very cold

Very cold

Rough

Rough

Rough

Rough

Wet

Tender

Moist

Harsh

Thick

Thick

Very thick

Very thick

Wrinkled

Very wrinkled

Having long hairs

Pale

Pale

Good

Clean

It becomes pale

It has long hairs

It becomes wrinkled with age

It becomes wrinkled here and there

It becomes warm

It becomes smooth

It becomes thick

It becomes fat

It becomes stretched

It droops

It hangs

It becomes ruddy

It becomes chili-red

It whitens

It becomes green

My flesh was torn off my index finger when I was eight.

Skin of my head

Skin of the face

Skin of the back

Skin of the abdomen

Skin of the hip

Skin of the thigh

Skin of the knee

Skin of the calf of the leg

Skin of the sole of the foot

Skin of the buttocks

Skin of our neck

Skin of our hand

Foreskin

Thick

Enveloping

My Flesh

Fleshiness

Clay

Earth

Our clay

Foundation

Our foundation

That which is foundation

Flesh of the head

Flesh of the face

Flesh of the lips

Flesh of the neck

Flesh of the chest

Flesh of our hip

Flesh of the thigh

Flesh of the knee

Flesh of the knee

Flesh of the face

Flesh of the face

Flesh of the face

My face

My face

My face

Flesh of the lips

Flesh of the neck

Flesh of the calf of the leg

Flesh of the ankle

Flesh of the sole of the foot

Flesh of the navel

Flesh of the palm of the hand

Flesh of the toe

Flesh of the finger

It becomes pale

It improves

It becomes clean

It becomes tender

It becomes tough

It becomes rough

It becomes black

It becomes brown

It becomes filthy

It becomes blotched

It evolves

It grows big

It enlarges

It becomes grease-stained

It becomes chili-red

It becomes pale

It becomes blue-green

It becomes firm

It becomes tender

It becomes lean

It bursts open

It heals

It becomes fat

It swells

It festers

It becomes damaged

It sickens

It becomes sick

It becomes tired

It is ripped

It is cut

It is pierced

It is split

It stretches

It becomes loose

It is resilient

It becomes hot

It becomes glowing hot

It becomes cold

It becomes cold

It droops

It is alive

It is alive

I am alive

It is living

It trembles

It quivers

It trembles

It shakes

It stinks

It shrinks

It is depressed

It shrinks

Thickness

My various thicknesses

Our thicknesses

Their thicknesses

Extensive

Thick

Thick

Flabby

Pale

Blood-flecked

Very bloody

Bloody

It becomes soft

Flabbiness

Flabbiness

Flabbiness

Flabbiness

Flabby

Flabby

My flabbiness

Our flabbiness

Flabbiness of our lips

Flabbiness of our chest

My flabbiness

Flabbiness of our neck

Flabbiness of the stomach

Greasy

Fatty

Heavy

Wet

Moist

It becomes grease-stained

Fat

My fat

Our fat

Their fat

Oily

Yellow

Fatty

Very yellow

Very yellow

Warm

Hot

Fat

Our fat

White

Soft

Compressible

Greasy

Very soft

Tissue

Our tissue

Our breast tissue

Brown

White

Green

Papery

Head

My head (that is to say the celestial part)

Our head

Our upper extremity

Little

Minute

Tiny

Big

Like a jar

Round

Broad

Toe-like

With eyes

With ears

With nose

With my . . .

Hair

It is black

Like charcoal

Like charcoal

Dark blue

Green

It forms

It becomes pointed

It becomes black

It becomes yellow

It becomes chili-red

It becomes bald

Forehead

Our forehead

Possessing with eminence

Bumpy

Very bumpy

Bulbous

Bare

Smooth

Smooth

Forehead wrinkles

Our forehead wrinkles

Very wrinkled

Very furrowed

Very furrowed

Eyelid

Cylindrical

Cylindrical

Cylindrical

Hairy

With eyebrow

Eyebrow

Hair

Fuzz

Black

Yellow

Ruddy

Fuzzy

Pointed at the end

Pointed at the end

Small

Orbit

Our orbit

EYE

Our eye

Mirror

My eye

Delicate

Soft

Round

Mano-shaped

Pestle-shaped

White

Yellow

Bright-eyed

Bright red

Transparent

Black

Clouded

Bowl-like
Blotched
It moves
It rolls
It wanders
It closes
It opens
With it there is seeing
There is seeing to the side
With it there is looking up
With it there is looking down
It recognizes people
It recognizes things
It sees
Whites of our eyes
Whites of my eyes
Whites of their eyes
Flesh
Full of nerves
Our iris
My iris
His iris
Her iris
Black
Transparent
Pupil of OUR eye
Our animated [organ]
Pupil of our eye
Transparent
Delicate
Very delicate
OUR COMPLETE MASTER
Torch

Light

Brilliance

Mirror

It illuminates one

It enlightens one

It leads one

It guides one

It sustains one

It becomes one

It becomes ailing

It decays

It becomes clouded

It becomes bow-like

It reduces

It roughens

It reduces

It becomes covered

It swells

It bursts open

A calcareous substance emerges

It becomes flesh-covered

It becomes filled with flesh

It becomes discolored

It becomes yellow

It sleeps

By means of it there is sleep

It is relaxed

It moves restlessly

Water runs

With it there is looking here and there

They become yellow

They have calcareous excretions

Ashen round clear

Our mirror
Instrument for seeing by
the esteemed
Guardian of honor
It illuminates
It illuminates one
It enlightens one

–REMIXED FROM THE FLORENTINE CODEX, 1548,

HAND UNKNOWN–

*

2011 Arizona Revised Statutes
Title 32. Professions and Occupations
32-1365.02: Authorizing agents; consent for
cremation, disinterment or embalming; **definition**

Universal Citation: AZ Rev Stat § 32-1365.02 (1996 through 1st Reg Sess 50th Legis)

A. Except as provided in section 32-1365.01 and in subsection E of this section, **it is unlawful** to cremate or disinter **a dead human body** without prior written consent of the authorizing agent.

B. Except as provided in section 32-1365.01, **it is unlawful** to embalm **a dead human body** without prior oral or written consent of the authorizing agent.

C. A funeral establishment shall create a written record of an oral consent given pursuant to this section that includes all of the following:

1. The name of the authorizing agent.

2. The relation of the authorizing agent to the deceased.

3. The date and time that consent was given.

4. The name of the person who obtained the consent.

5. Any other information required by the board.

D. In determining who the proper authorizing agent is, the order of preference is the same as provided in section 36-831. If there is more than one member in a category listed in section 36-831 entitled to serve as the authorizing agent, final arrangements may be made by any member of that category unless that member knows of an objection by another member of the category. If an objection is known, final arrangements shall be made by a majority of the members of the category who are reasonably available.

E. On the order of a court or a county medical examiner, or a person performing the duties of a county medical examiner, a dead human body shall be disinterred.

F. If none of the persons listed in section 36-831 is willing or financially capable of providing for the cremation or embalming of a dead human body, the public fiduciary or other person who is designated by the county in which a death occurs to handle funeral arrangements may order the cremation or embalming.

G. A funeral establishment, an employee or agent of a funeral establishment or a licensee shall exercise due diligence to obtain the consent required pursuant to this section from the proper authorizing agent. It is an affirmative defense to any action or claim brought against a crematory, cemetery or funeral establishment relating to the disposition of **a dead human body** that the crematory, cemetery or funeral establishment relied in good faith on the direction of a person who claimed to be the authorizing agent in providing for the lawful disposition of **a dead human body**. The decision of a crematory, cemetery or funeral establishment to cremate or otherwise provide for the lawful disposition of **a dead human body** in reliance on the direction of a person who claims to be the authorizing agent is presumed to be in good faith unless the crematory, cemetery or funeral establishment has actual knowledge that the claim is false.

H. If the authorizing agent is not reasonably available or **unable to act** as the authorizing agent, **the person's** right to be the authorizing agent **shall pass to the next** person or **category of persons** in the order of preference prescribed in section 36-831.

I. It is presumed that the authorizing agent is not reasonably available to act as authorizing agent if the crematory, cemetery or funeral establishment **after exercising** due diligence has been unable to contact the individual or if that person has been unwilling or unable to make final arrangements for the disposition of the decedent within fifteen days after the initial contact by the crematory, cemetery or funeral establishment. If a person in a prior category makes an initial contact with the crematory, cemetery or funeral establishment or becomes able before the final disposition of the decedent, that person resumes **that person's right** to serve as the authorizing agent.

J. Any dispute among any of the persons listed in section 36-831, subsection A concerning the right **to control** the disposition, including cremation, of a decedent's remains shall be resolved by **the parties** to the dispute or by a court of competent jurisdiction in order to expedite the resolution of a dispute among the parties. A crematory, cemetery or funeral establishment shall not be liable for refusing to accept the decedent's remains or inter, cremate or otherwise dispose of a decedent's remains until it receives a court order or other suitable confirmation that the dispute has been resolved or settled. A crematory, cemetery or funeral establishment may bring an action in a court of competent jurisdiction in order to expedite the resolution of a dispute among the parties listed in section 36-831, subsection A.

K. For the purposes of this section "reasonably available" means a person who is able to be contacted by the crematory, cemetery or funeral establishment without undue effort and who is willing and able to act within fifteen days after the initial contact by the crematory, cemetery or funeral establishment.

*

*Pima County in Arizona now cremates all its undocumented dead human bodies.

*The ashes of 35 John Does—at least some believed to be illegal border crossers—and 31 others whose dead human bodies went unclaimed are now in a new columbarium at the county cemetery.

*The county expects another probable 300 dead human border crossers to be cremated soon.

*As of Monday, the Pima County Medical Examiner's Office had the remains of about 155 unidentified dead human border crossers in its morgue. They will be ashes by the Monday following, per AZ 32-1365.

*In 2016 the Vatican decreed the new guidelines for cremation. The ashes must be kept in a "sacred place" and they should not be divided among the family members or turned into decorative objects.

BOOK XI
Earthly Things

Make comparisons

A compendium

Created through

a
                                    teotl

a

        {term}

a

        thing good and evil

a sun

a god

a rich storehouse

of all

meaning

SIGN

Opaque silhouettes of Mexican undocumented immigrants haunted the I-5 corridor between Mexico and California for decades. Serving as a documented warning to motorists of the possibility of immigrants crossing the highway, the "immigrant sign" hid the reality that hundreds of immigrants had been killed on the highways in the late 1980s. Instead of California dealing with the real tragedy of the deaths that were caused by unjust immigration policies, Caltrans felt it necessary to post a traffic sign that would warn motorists of Mexicans darting across the highway. I find out that the sign was created by

John Hood, a Navajo Caltrans employee, who based the sign's male likeness on César Chávez and used the image of the family and child with pigtails in order to elicit empathy from the driving public. He also noted that the three Mexican family members' plight is similar to that of the Navajo on the Long Walk in 1864. I wonder, does this change its intended *effect*?

Caltrans didn't say whether the signs were successful; that is, whether deaths stopped occurring on the stretch of highway where they were erected. Operation Gatekeeper took effect and the undocumented were forced to make their own "long walk" from the highways to the desert, where their deaths would be hidden from the public eye and buried by the sands. The last of the signs disappeared in September of 2018 under mysterious circumstances. Caltrans claims not to have dismantled them, but the signs' difficult-to-reach locations allow few explanations for their disappearance. In the end, it all turns out to be inconsequential; the signs will not be replaced as the program has ended. Mexicans no longer pose a threat to California's citizen motorists.

Two months after the last sign disappeared from the highway, Caltrans began selling off their stock of the remaining signs. I find a sign on eBay along with hundreds of T-shirts, mugs, posters, and key chains that depict the sign's likeness. I win the auction: $124.99 for a "real authentic Caltrans immigrant sign used on the border, which may have blemishes on it since it was a real sign." The sign is 30″ x 20″. I am not sure why I buy it. Buying off all the old Caltrans stock in hopes that it will never be put up again is an exercise in futility. I hang it in my office at the university. "That is so cool," students and colleagues tell me when they enter. "Is that real?" "Yes, it is a real sign," I tell them.

MOLCAJETE

There was a child went forth every day, / And the first object he look'd upon, that object he became.

-WALT WHITMAN-

It is important to point out that at its core, the *Florentine Codex*, originally titled *La Historia universal de las cosas de Nueva España* (*The Universal History of the Things of New Spain*), is a work that spends much of its time documenting things. As the title suggests, the compilers knew that things—their history, their composition, their use value—are what makes a people, and they are what stands as the trace of the people's existence. Writing at the end of their material existence, through image and word, the compilers catalogued a world of material things that were slipping from their grasp. The compilers rendered things both as material objects that constituted their lived identity and as ethereal metonyms for their vanishing world. In stark opposition to the "atomist" teachings of Lucretius, whose work *The Nature of Things* stood as a materialist foundation for the "thinking of things in the universe" during the period in which Sahagún would write, for the codex things are metaphysical; they hold the ghosts of the past within their atoms, released into our lived existence with each touch as mnemonic specters. The inscribing, making, and using of things are haunting acts that transform things from solely named, documented material objects into objects that hold the memories of those who touched them, of those who used them, of those who are now dead. Things lie among us as ghosts and mediate the relationship between the living and the dead; they are the mediums that enable us to call upon the lost voices to enter our lives.

*

Slovenian philosopher Slavoj Žižek spoke of the haunting nature of things in a ghost story he told me years ago. During a visit to Boulder he retold this tale about a friend whose wife died in a tragic car accident. This friend was gifted a pen by his wife the morning of her death, and to Žižek's bewilderment, the man never wept or mourned the passing of his wife. At the funeral he stood stoic, silent. And for years afterward this man never mourned. Never missed his wife. His antidote to grief and longing: he would carry the pen with him at every moment, caressing it between his fingers as if it held the spirit of his wife within the ink receptacle. One morning, however, he awoke to find the pen had disappeared from his nightstand. He frantically tore his house apart, only to finally realize he could not find it anywhere—it had vanished while he slept. Later that same day while at work he had a nervous breakdown and was institutionalized. His wife, to him, had finally died when he lost the pen, and her memory was lost forever. Her specter had vanished.

*

I have one thing that holds the ghosts of my Mexican past: a century-old *molcajete* that my grandmother gave me as a wedding gift when I got married. This object connects me not only to my past but also to the Mexicas of the *Florentine Codex*, as the *molcajete* is shown in numerous images and described in many places.

I must confess, though, I have not thought about this object since it was given to me in 1996. Though I use it occasionally to break up cumin seed for rice or beans, it does not have the evocative pull on me that it should. It wasn't until I kept seeing it in the *Florentine Codex* that I called my grandmother to find out more about it.

I call when my mother is in Houston with her for a family reunion. They put me on speakerphone, and I unsuccessfully dance with them, trying to lead in the direction of answers that will help me understand why I was given this *molcajete* when she has four daughters who cook better than I do. "How are you, Grandmother?" "Fine, *hijo*, just starting to feel old, my mind and body just feel so old." At nearly ninety, she still looks like she is in her sixties. My mother too defies age. "I'm sorry, Grandmother." I try to change the subject quickly. I hate hearing about age-related health issues. My heart begins to skip beats. "Grandmother, how was the reunion?" My mom chimes in, "It was great. All the cousins were there, and they had great BBQ, not Mikeska's though. But El Campo, it is so sad, it is a ghost town." "Yes, *hijo*," my grandmother agrees, "a ghost town. I was sad, *hijo*, everyone is dead now and it was kind of lonely." "I'm sorry, grandmother." I try to change the subject. "Grandmother, can you tell me about the *molcajete* you gave me? Why did you give it to me?" "Well, *hijo*, your great-grandmother Lola, Dolores, gave me it on my wedding day fifty years before your wedding, in 1946. Didn't I tell you that, *hijo*? You, me, and your great-grandmother got married the same day fifty years apart. Your great-grandmother brought it from Saltillo, Mexico, when she was younger, when she immigrated here from Mexico, *hijo*; she brought it all the way from Mexico for me, *hijo*, for you, and I gave it to you. You know she was the last immigrant from Mexico in our family, *hijo*; she did not get her papers until she was in her fifties. I think she was born in 1888, when you could go back and forth much more easily." "Grandmother, why is there a chunk out of it, did you drop it?" "Well, *hijo*, that is a long story, you need to come see me, and I will tell you what happened. It is a good story, *hijo*." My mom interjects, "Mom, that happened with Daddy and his brother, who died decades ago, when they came home drunk one night and wanted huevos rancheros and you dropped it cooking for them. It woke me up. I remember like it was yesterday. That damn thing weighs a ton." "No, *hija*, that is not when it happened. *Hijo*, you need to come see me before I am gone, then I won't be able to tell you the story about it. *Hijo*, you have to know all the stories and I'll teach you some more recipes." "I will try, Grandmother."

BOOK XII
Conquest

I desired to write in the Mexican language

For these reasons, it seems to me to have written this history,

A time it is believed

I

Did
Not

tell the truth

DESERT

This nostalgic memory of my desert past has faded into another's eye, spoken with another tongue. I now see that the desert erases the undocumented and tastes of iron, resembling the flavor of blood. Its sands form an unmapped mausoleum, where heat and wind turn bodies into voiceless traces without papers buried in the torrid land. My view of the desert reemerged in the summer of 2018 when I heard my name on the news. "The body was found in a hollow concrete pillar in Lancaster, California. It is not confirmed, but his name may be Rivera, and his residence is still unknown." They break away to a picture of a column in front of the entrance of a supermarket, with makeshift crosses in the distance. I recognize the supermarket where they pulled out his body; it is just three miles from where I grew up. The body was undiscovered for days. TV anchors and comment boards surmise that he must have been an undocumented immigrant. "His body was so badly decomposed that he was oozing out of the concrete pillar" at WinCo on West Avenue K. The desert takes another unknown Mexican life.

I spent my teenage years in Lancaster, a hot, windy High Desert bedroom community about fifty miles outside of Los Angeles. The weather and land were harsh. I never found the landscape of the desert beautiful like so many writers and artists. My mom and I moved there from North Hollywood when she got a job in aerospace. I missed L.A. every day that I lived in Lancaster. So, for me, the desert is a barren, lonely, sand-infused space where wind cuts through your body and turns your skin into cracked leather and your eye sockets into dry batholiths. I remember when I truly learned of the power of this desert, its ability to break down the body, to wither the soul into sand crystals. Over thirty years ago, the summer before I left Lancaster forever, my car broke down in Lake L.A. (a touch deeper into the desert of Lancaster) during a 122-degree day in August. Back then you could be there for hours with no cars in sight, seeing no homes, no gas stations, and no water or food stops. After I drove the wrong way down a dirt road off the highway and broke down with nothing in sight, in one hour my body began to shut down; a deep headache was quickly turning into heat hallucinations and panic. For an hour there was not a car in sight. Should I walk down the road, stay put? The sun, wind, and sand engulfed my body, evaporating any moisture or life within an hour. Minutes before I was going to start to walk, an old salvage tow truck passed me and pulled over. A thin, tall Latino, around fifty, got out of the truck and slowly walked up. "*¿Necesitas ayuda?*" "*Sí, sí, gracias,*" I replied. I suspect that upon hearing my broken Spanish he realized it would be easier to communicate if he replied in English: "Mr. Duran, who lives on the other side of the ridge, called about someone on the road. He watches over this valley," he said. "He thought he would be coming to another dead body. You are lucky I was headed to Lake L.A. to the salvage yard to get parts when I heard him on the CB," he said, "or I would not have been out this way for hours. I found bodies out here once, in a car. Why were you even out here?" he asked. "Going to the junkyard too," I replied, "looking for parts for my Ghia, and when I left, I went right instead of left and by the time I realized it I broke down." "Bet you won't do that again. *Estúpido . . . estúpido niño.*" I agreed but stayed silent.

There would be no reenacting the movie *Grand Canyon* here. He and I did not connect like Danny Glover and Kevin Kline, and I did not find some wisdom in my act of stupidity, which was built on an arrogant failure to really understand the power of the desert before that moment. Then, I was just embarrassed and too scared and young to really know what could have happened. Now, it's one of those moments you think back on and realize that at one time in your life you could have died. Or maybe I could have walked and found a house, who knows? Years later in college I told the story a couple times trying to humorously describe where I was from. "The desert could have killed me," I would laugh. Now, though, I do not laugh or take this event lightly—or the desert, for that matter. My hour in the desert still makes me realize I can only imagine what Raymundo Rivera went through, or the thousands of other Mexicans who have been held by the desert because they are searching for papers on the other side of a border. I have to imagine, as I am not trying to flee oppressive governments or unjust economic systems because I do not have papers, searching for water in a desert, hoping that a sip will help me walk one more mile and maybe, just maybe, make it over a border. I survived, escaped, and left Lancaster one month later when I was seventeen. I had my papers and the desert had to let me go. Raymundo Rivera, whom they would identify a week after the discovery of his body, was not so lucky. He was trying to elude the cops and must have fallen from the supermarket's roof into the hollow pillar of dried sand, where he would eventually overheat, die, and slowly decompose. He was entombed there for a week, the coroners would later surmise.

I return to Lancaster three months after they find Rivera's body to bury my father-in-law. Between the wake and the funeral, I go to the place where Rivera's body was found, just blocks from where my in-laws live. The crosses are gone, and there's not a mark in the recently repaired concrete pillar. It is as if he never died there, the only trace of him in newspaper archives or the GoFundMe campaign the family started in order to help retrieve and transport his body. That night I stand in the desert behind my mother-in-law's house. I think back to when I broke down, not having thought about it in years. Maybe it is the confluence of my father-in-law's wake and Raymundo Rivera's tomb being so close, but I feel—I now know—that if you listen hard enough you find that the quiet of the desert is full of the screams of the dead, trying to be heard and identified. I stare out at the sand and listen. I recall aloud a stanza from Lorna Dee Cervantes's poem "Blind Desert Snakes":

> Across the immigrant road, wisps of ice
> Knot and unknot sinews of light and water,
> Water the parched mouths crave. The voiceless
> Snakes of a voiceless race wage across the desert
> Landscapes. An empty field waits for the wake.
> Blind desert snakes, the sinuous ghosts of the ones
> Gone down unreel: the young man left behind, the wan
> Girl taken and raped. The scratched-out eyes of freedom
> Shrivel at the weight. Dignity's dried arroyos
> Wait for the spring of our change. Give it. ¡Justicia!

*

CADA DIA MUEREN TRES PERSONAS EN
LA FRONTERA. NUNCA ES EL COYOTE.

Hace más de cuatro días	*It has been more than four days*
que vaga por el desierto.	*that he wanders in the desert.*
Otro se quedó en la línea	*Another one died at the border line*
y adelante un futuro incierto.	*and facing him is an uncertain future.*
Cerró sus ojos y soltó el aliento	*He closed his eyes and gave his last breath*
como quien pierde por fin la batalla	*like one who has finally lost the battle*
... Recé y lloré por mi amigo muerto	*... I prayed and I cried for my dead friend*
pa' que su pena no pase en vano.	*so that his suffering would not be in vain.*
Después de llorar me sentí más valiente	*After I cried I felt more fearless*
y juré nuevamente ante la cruz de madera.	*and swore again in front of the wooden cross.*
Volveré a mi pueblo allá con mi gente	*I will return to my hometown with my people*
Y no habrá más cruces en la frontera.	*And there will be no more crosses at the border.*

Excerpted from *Migra Corridos*, produced and funded by ICE (Department of Homeland Security), and performed by Rodolfo Hernández. The United States spends an unknown amount of appropriated monies producing the album *Migra Corridos*, and a website,

https://www.dvidshub.net/publication/749/no-mas-cruces-en-la
-frontera, in order to better communicate the dangers of crossing the
desert. The program is quietly defunded shortly after the CD's release.

✳

What threat did these women and girls pose that they were the target of such brutal violence against their bodies? These completely powerless bodies . . . who worked ten-hour shifts . . . who lived in hovels made of maquiladora scrap in the middle of the desert . . . who had their reproductive cycles under surveillance . . . who got fired for being pregnant . . . what threat did they pose? And whose job was it to keep that threat under control?

-ALICIA GASPAR DE ALBA, *DESERT BLOOD: THE JUÁREZ MURDERS*-

Since the publication of *Desert Blood*, over ten thousand documented women are still missing or presumed dead, lost to the desert. The continued disappearance of women forces the hand of the Juárez government to create an app, No Estoy Sola, to help combat this humanitarian crisis, one that governments have denied for decades. The problem: there is very little cell phone reception in the desert where the bodies disappear, and maquiladora workers can't afford cell phone services, or, if they manage to, the companies confiscate their phones. They remain lost to the desert, hidden from invisible hands that search for them in vain with a compass programmed in Java.

*

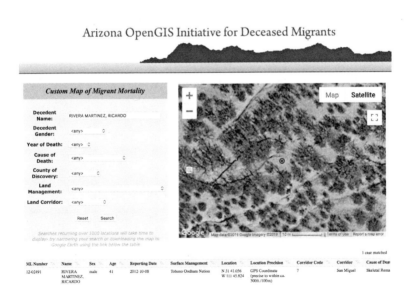

I search the "death map" for any Riveras. There are six identifiable Riveras among the thousands of undocumented bodies found in the desert. Since the death map was commissioned, there have been over three thousand bodies discovered and their graves identified by GPS, a pixelated cross added to mark a life lost in the desert. A recent study has found that there are tens of thousands of unmarked ghosts who wander outside the map, outside of GPS. Even Homeland Security estimates that there are over six thousand. I stare at the screen showing the six Riveras found. I hear nothing. Is this *"justicia"*? Being found and turned into a number and a red coordinate blip on the death map? Is it enough simply to locate the dead? Are they marked by crosses in the desert, or is this it—a virtual mausoleum marked with an invisible hand?

CLIMATE

Rendered in John Gast's portrait in 1872, the doppelganger of Manifest Destiny still feeds off the soil made from the bones of the dead. Millions are buried within the earth of the Americas that we all walk on, that we all cultivate. We farm, drill, and build into dirt infused with the blood and skin of my ancestors, so many dead bodies that our climate changes, our weather affected by every lost breath. The lingering specter of Manifest Destiny's hold on the climate of the Americas was finally made manifest in 2019, the same week when, reportedly, "holes in the polar vortex" were allowing record-breaking weather systems to escape the Arctic region into North America and plunge some areas to −56 degrees (Fahrenheit). Two studies about global warming's profound effects on Latinx communities, both living and dead, were made public. The first was a study on the climate of the sixteenth-century Americas, when Sahagún wrote the *Florentine Codex*—the period, the study concludes, when there were so many Mesoamerican deaths that the earth's climate actually changed. An estimated 56 million Mesoamericans were wiped off the planet in the name of Manifest Destiny and the ice at the earth's poles would forever be changed. By the time the first major stages of conquest were complete in 1610, the earth's temperature had changed enough to label that period "the Little Ice Age." I watch the report being packaged on CNN, between reports on how eggs can be frozen on the sidewalk in Minneapolis, as they state what Latinxs have known for generations before the study of ice core samples. "The really weird thing is, the depopulation of the Americas may have inadvertently allowed the Europeans to dominate the world," says UCL geography professor Mark Maslin. "It also allowed for the Industrial Revolution and for Europeans to continue that domination," he concludes. "So weird," I respond to the TV, as a map is flashed on the screen:

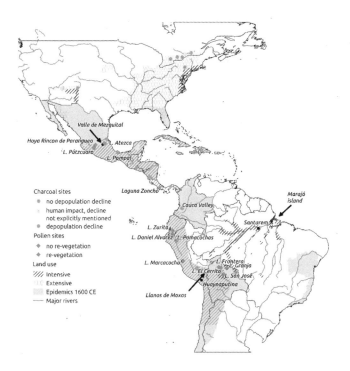

Charcoal sites
- no depopulation decline
- human impact, decline not explicitly mentioned
- depopulation decline

Pollen sites
- no re-vegetation
- re-vegetation

Land use
- Intensive
- Extensive
- Epidemics 1600 CE
- Major rivers

A week later environmentalists are up in arms about the fact that President Trump did not say the word "climate" in his State of the Union speech, but they were not troubled by him arguing that the border is swarming and infested with dangerous immigrants and we must build a wall or face another government shutdown. The next day environmentalists are arguing that weather shifts in Mexico have caused drought and deforestation and led to Mexican and Indigenous people migrating and searching for work and water. Global warming will affect the climate to such a degree that in the coming decades migration will increase as erratic weather patterns become the norm. The reports do not lament the dislocation of Latinx peoples but rather the fact that immigration will become an even larger problem and more undocumented people will try to enter the United States. The earth will suffer, as will our borders, and the taxpayers will bear the costs. Maybe this, they strategize, will get Trump to use the word "climate."

Years before this, I give a talk at the Chautauqua Center in Boulder, Colorado, on immigration and the browning of America, exploring the complicated and fruitful ways that this browning will affect everyone. The climate of the audience is affable; the entire audience is white, affluent, and geriatric, so I give pithy anecdotes about how salsa is overtaking ketchup as the condiment of choice in the United States. The talk is safe, bland, and boring, just what my hosts wanted. A safe celebration of Latino diversity. After the usual questions about Mexican food during the question and answer session, someone tells me that Mexican immigration is killing the planet. He cites the Sierra Club's positions and global warnings that immigration is bad for the earth's climate. "Shouldn't we be talking about the death of the earth rather than the browning of it?" "We should talk about both," I say; "they are interrelated. But I am not going to place the blame for climate change on the backs of Mexican immigrants. Are you?" He responds, "The earth is what we need to save. The planet is my priority . . . It should be all of ours." The hosts look nervous and abruptly end the Q and A: "Give our guest Professor Rivera a hand." Claps ensue. I wonder now if he has read the report about Mesoamerican deaths and "the Little Ice Age" in the sixteenth century. Does he understand that the report reveals that European expansion was the original sin against that male fantasy "Mother Nature," Manifest Destiny's iconic doppelganger? That European expansion and its destructive wake, turning bodies into disposable garbage in the lands of the New World, led to the first great man-made climate event? What John Jota Leaños renders so well is that Manifest Destiny still hides, waits, hovering as a memento mori in the clouds of blame and ignorance. We have come full circle, and CNN covers every change in temperature.

WALLS

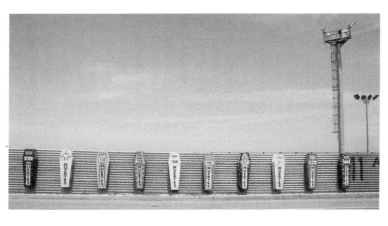

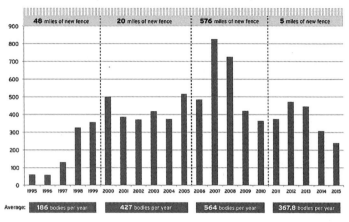

Body Count Rises With US-Mexico Border Fence Construction

Border fence data: U.S. Customs and Border Protection. Body count data: Mexico's Foreign Affairs Ministry, UC San Diego's Center for Comparative Immigration Studies and U.S. Customs and Border Protection.

KPBS

They need a barrier. They need a wall. If you don't have it, it's going to be nothing but hard work and grueling problems, and, by the way, and death. And death. A lot of death.

–DONALD TRUMP, 2019–

✳

I built walls with the absent words of my father. The first bricks were laid when he emotionally left my mother and me when I was three, and my mother and I would flee the patriarchal walls of Texas to never truly return. In the decades that followed, we peeked at each other from either side of a self-imposed barrier, never really knowing how to cross. Yearly visits became weekly calls, while hearing my mother fighting with him over the years about child support, then the physical absences turned into monthly calls. My father and I talk today, monthly usually, but of the mundane, and about my daughter, whom he has not seen in thirteen years.

The last parts of the wall are solidified when I see him fall down the stairs having a heart attack when he is fifty-three. Landing on cold white tile, his face empty, his color sucked out of him. Staring over his body, I don't think to do CPR; I slap him in the face to wake him up, thinking he passed out from exhaustion or low blood sugar. My first panic attack happens that night. Watching him roll down the stairs into a fetal ball, unresponsive, dead, I realized that the end, or death, was neither elegant nor romantic. It was physical, visceral, confused, and loud. Death would haunt me for decades after this moment. He would haunt me. He died for a few minutes, he would tell me during the recovery weeks that followed. I saw you over me, he would say. I told him I did not want to talk about it. I couldn't tell him I think about his death every day. About my death now. We talk about everything but ourselves. The last section of the wall is complete.

> Son, you say you want to put up a fence in your backyard, but you do not support a border wall. That is hypocritical. Why do you have the right to secure your possessions while the government has no right to put up its own fence? President Trump is trying to save us all.

> Dad, I'm not going to go into the major ways your anecdote is a false equivalency, but I do want to say that you do remember that our families are immigrants, right? And that all of them had to cross walls to get here. All of us at one time or another were undocumented. You said you did ancestry DNA, right? There are no such Houston peoples we were descendants of.

Son, no one hopped over a fence. We came here the right way. You know Obama has a big wall around his house, right? I bet the taxpayers are paying for that one.

Dad, our families picked cotton and cultivated rice in Texas fields. They were not citizens. How do you forget these things? Did you know that Obama had more threats on his life than all other presidents combined? Dad, I am not going to ask everyone who visits for their papers, or shoot them, or separate families, or ask my Italian neighbors to build my wall. I am just trying to make sure Winnie does not get out when I leave her out for the day. That dog runs whenever she gets a chance.

Son, that is crazy. Slow down. We need a wall. It is getting crazy here in Houston. Gangs everywhere. Drugs in all of the schools. You remember poor Joshua Wilkerson, boy down in Pearland? He was murdered by a DACA. You don't know what it's like in Texas.

Dad, where does your wall end?

He is quiet, and the conversation, in which we debate politics, concluding in the same way three or four different times over the months, is over in seven minutes. Nearly all the calls are seven minutes long. How did a Mexican man become so afraid of himself, of his people? Maybe fear is inherited. Maybe this is why I fear my own death? Why I get uncontrollable PVCs? Fear of returning to Texas, of seeing him. Every year I tell my daughter we are going to visit; I'm going to take her to see him before he dies. *We are getting old, son, the whole family is getting old, we will all be gone soon*, he told me a few months back. I tell him I will be there, just not this year. There are just too many walls on the way back to Texas.

POSTLUDE

AN INQUIRY ON THE EDGE OF TOMORROW

Will I be granted an afterlife? I ask this question while sitting in the archives of the Laurentian Library, the library Michelangelo designed, and where, like me, Georges Bataille would read the *Florentine Codex*. My second time here I am finally allowed to see the last book, *The Conquest*, and think about the end days of my ancestors. Were they given an afterlife? Will I see the people that I have been studying for so long in this afterlife? Sahagún prayed to God that his codex would grant him the privilege of an afterlife, after documenting the Mexica people whom his own culture would help destroy. My mind traces the path the *Florentine Codex* took to Italy from Mexico, and I am taken from this monument of the Enlightenment to the Mesoamerican ruins of the goddess Ixchel in Mexico on the Isla Mujeres. By a thousand-year-old stone structure crumbling thirteen miles from the resorts that litter the coast of the Yucatán Peninsula, I show my passport to a government official before I enter the ruins and am given a wristband that "must be worn at all times under risk of prosecution or deportation." The wristband's number corresponds with the number on my passport document to ensure that I do not loot the ruins. Like many before me, however, I enter the ruins only to take the document off my wrist and tie it to the altar of Ixchel, a sacrifice for my eternity. Meditating at the edge of Mexico's haunted Mesoamerican past while peering into a fathomless gulf, I am undocumented for one fleeting moment. I close my eyes and imagine myself walking off the page.

NOTES

*A note on the prefaces to each book in this volume. These are erasures from the *Florentine Codex*'s author prefaces, the only place where Sahagún addresses his audience and his authorial intent. I want to thank Roberto Tejada for helping me realize this project through the publication of these prefaces in *Mandorla* years ago.

PRELUDE–AN INQUIRY: HOW DO YOU DOCUMENT THE UNDOCUMENTED?

I want to thank Cristina Rivera Garza for helping me work through the idea of necropoetics. The conversation I had with her at the 2019 Cross Borders event, hosted by myself and Julia Carr, in Boulder, Colorado, led me to think through the ways in which poetics, specters, and the necropolitical merge. See also her book The Restless Dead: Necrowriting and Disappropriation.

6   "self-preservation . . ." The quotations in this paragraph are from d'Alembert, Preliminary Discourse.
7   "The life of civilized peoples . . ." Bataille, "Extinct America."
8   "There must be some answers in the shadows . . ." Teresa Margolles, "Interview Teresa Margolles, Artist," by Moira Jeffrey, *The Scotsman*, April 17, 2012, https://www.scotsman.com/arts-and-culture/interview-teresa-margolles-artist-2463493.

10 *"an assemblage, a montage . . ."* Anzaldúa, *Borderlands.*

11 *Zweite Enzyklopädie von Tlön.* See http://tloen-enzyklopaedie.de/e _texts/texts.htm.

11 *"what Georges Bataille calls the spéculaire . . ."* For an interesting discussion of images and phantasmatology in Bataille, see Gasché, *Georges Bataille,* 111–22.

13 "leaves of Leviticus and Judges . . ." Plascencia, *People of Paper,* 13–15.

14 "that treaty, according to Juan Gómez-Quiñones, is a foundational document . . ." Gómez-Quiñones, *Roots of Chicano Politics.*

15 "A Bill." The base text quoted and erased here is the Reforming American Immigration for a Strong Economy Act, S. 1103, 116th Congress (2019–20), https://www.congress.gov/bill/116th-congress/ senate-bill/1103/text.

20 "memento mori that enable participation in another's mortality." Sontag, *On Photography.*

CONJUNTO

In 1939, the WPA transcribed and recorded a particularly important corrido, "The Wet-Back," in Sarita, Texas. Flaco Jiménez would later record a variation of this song as "Un Mojado Sin Licencia" (1955). Coincidentally, 1939 was the same year that Flaco Jiménez was born in San Antonio.

EDUCATION

The base text used for the erasure in this section is the 1947 appeals court ruling from the court case *Mendez v. Westminster.* See https://law.justia .com/cases/federal/appellate-courts/F2/161/774/1566460/.

APOCALYPSE 2012

101 *"Anxiety is there . . ."* Heidegger, *What Is Metaphysics?*

(HANGING) TREES

The list of names of lynched Mexicans is remixed and edited from the amazing book *Lynching in the West 1850–1935*, by Ken Gonzales-Day. I exhumed the names from the exhaustive list that is in his book; some of the names are not complete or exact due to the nature of the archive.

AMEXICA

118 "[Mexicans] are willing to do . . ." See Office of the Press Secretary, "Presidents Bush, Fox Discuss State Visit Remarks by President George Bush and President Vicente Fox of Mexico Upon Departure," White House website, September 6, 2001, https://georgewbush -whitehouse.archives.gov/news/releases/2001/09/20010906-6.html.

INTERLUDE–*AN INQUIRY INTO THE "MEXICAN QUESTION"*

126 "overspread and to possess the whole of our continent . . ." O'Sullivan, "Annexation," 234–35.

129 "race is the key to much that seems obscure . . ." This and other quotations in the paragraph are from Cushing, "Mexico," 343–45.

130 "It marked America's first intimate exposure . . ." Johannsen, *To the Halls of the Montezumas*, 12.

130 "exotic and foreign manners . . ." See Johannsen, *To the Halls of the Montezumas*, 34–73.

131 "A widely publicized 1848 study undertaken by a Cincinnati phrenologist . . ." This study is found in *Niles National Register* 70 (June 1848), p. 68.

131 "as Martha Menchaca and Deena González have argued . . ." See Menchaca, *Recovering History, Constructing Race*; and González, "Treaty of Guadalupe Hidalgo."

132 "Gómez-Quiñones makes this point . . ." See Gómez-Quiñones, *Roots of Chicano Politics.*

132 "as Norma Alarcón astutely theorizes . . ." See Alarcón, "Chicana Feminism."

133 "How did it happen that over Texas . . ." Engels, "Democratic Pan-Slavism." Translation into English by the Marx-Engels Institute.

134 "that Mexicans were 'degenerate' . . ." Marx, "Intervention in Mexico."

134 "a motley amalgamation of impure races . . ." This and other quotations in the paragraph are from Calhoun, Statement to Congress.

HOMO DOCUMENTATOR

151 *"There is no document of civilization . . ."* Benjamin, "Theses on the Philosophy of History," 254.

151 *"A document [now] is . . . through registration."* Ferraris, *Documentality,* 2–4.

151 *"Naked life is . . . (. . . a branch of geology)."* Ferraris, *Documentality,* 358–62.

151 *"The representation of the mind . . . (. . . to at least two persons)."* Ferraris, *Documentality,* 13, 145–48.

152 *"Documents can have . . . rationalist philosophical outlook."* Riles, *Documents,* 9–11.

152 *"A document—be it a book . . . what we humans are."* Levy, *Scrolling Forward,* 7–9.

152 *"Documentation was a set of techniques . . . formulated in these terms."* Buckland, "What Is a 'Document'?"

153 *"Document   Any source of information . . . as an authority."* Briet, *Qu'est-ce que la documentation?*

153 *"Examples   manuscripts . . . aesthetics and phenomenology."* Buckland, "What Is a 'Document'?"

153 *"A document is the repository . . . really irrational variety."* Duyvis, *Normalisatie op het gebied der documentatie.*

154 *"A document is something . . . processes of biological evolution."* Smith, "How to Do Things with Documents," 181.

154 *"To be governed is to be . . . every moment."* Pierre-Joseph Proudhon, "Idée générale de la révolution au XIXème siècle," quoted in Caplan and Torpey, "Introduction."

155 *"The creation of a 'legible people' . . . and customers."* Caplan and Torpey, "Introduction," 6–7.

155 *"One set of questions . . . represent who we 'are."'* Dardy, *Identités de papiers*, quoted in Caplan and Torpey, "Introduction," and additionally translated/remixed by the author.

DEAD LANGUAGE

159 *"Some Coyotes are saying . . ."* The poem by the unknown Nahuatl author is quoted from León-Portilla, *Broken Spears*.

SANTA MUERTE

166 *"We know it is true . . ."* Poem remixed from León-Portilla, *Broken Spears*.

169 "represents a very real enemy . . ." Lorentzen, *"Santa Muerte."*

THE PICKING DEAD

174 *"Farmworkers are exposed to pesticides in a variety of ways . . ."* The 2013 report by Farmworker Justice quoted here can be found at https://kresge.org/sites/default/files/Exposed-and-ignored-Farmworker-Justice-KF.pdf.

DAY OF THE DEAD©

179 *"Coco,* Scene The Border of the Dead." The brief scene from the movie *Coco* (Pixar Animation Studios, 2017) was transcribed and set in screenplay format by the author.

183 "spent so much time and research . . ." Mark Snetiker, "How the Pixar Animators Solved Pixar's Big Bony Challenge," *Entertainment Weekly*, November 13, 2017.

MASCULINITY

197 "Four centuries from the discovery of America . . ." Turner, *Frontier in American History*, 62.

197 "Moreover, as Mark Seltzer reminds us . . ." Seltzer, *Bodies and Machines*, 56.

199 "[my] blood relations . . ." Quoted in the *Las Vegas Optic*, 1897.

200 "dime novels specifically devoted to . . ." Tatum, *Inventing Billy the Kid*, 61–64.

201 "the Anglo-Saxon civilization was destined . . ." Hough, *Story of the Outlaw*, 307.

202 "pure fiction wholly devoid of fact." Otero, *Real Billy the Kid*, 34–35.

209 "Act 1." A large part of this section is quoted from Anaya, *Billy the Kid*.

RESURRECTION

215 "Review of the Los Angeles County Sheriff's Department's Investigation . . ." This section is quoted and remixed from the special report by the Los Angeles County Office of Independent Review, which is posted on the Los Angeles Sheriff's Department website http://shq.lasdnews.net/shq/LASD_Oversight/Report%20on%20the %20Sheriff%27s%20Department%27s%20Investigation%20into%20 the%20Homicide%20of%20Ruben%20Salazar.pdf.

PURGATORY (MICTLĀN)

223 "I have gained a lot of weight . . ." The words of Araceli Velásquez quoted in this paragraph are from Sara Fleming, "Eleven Months into Sanctuary, Araceli Velásquez Speaks Out Against Immigration

Policy," *Westword*, July 11, 2018; and Joel Dyer, "Windows, Walls, and Invisible Lines   Araceli Velásquez," *Boulder Weekly*, October 4, 2018.

POSSESSION

226   "No experience in *Carne y arena* . . ." Alejandro González Iñárritu, artist's statement, *Carne y arena* website, https://carne-y-arena.com/ About.

226   "This takes us back . . ." Benjamin B, "*Carne y Arena* Part 2 N o t e s on VR Cinema Design," *TheFilmBook* (blog), *American Cinematographer*, June 30, 2017, https://ascmag.com/blog/the-film-book/carne-y -arena-notes-on-vr-cinema.

226   "a fusion of identities arises . . ." Quoted in "Alejandro G. Iñárritu CARNE y ARENA," press release, Artsy (website), n.d., https://www .artsy.net/show/fondazione-prada-alejandro-g-inarritu-carne-y -arena.

PHANTOM LIMBS

The italicized passages at the beginning of this section are remixed by the author from Prieto, "Glorious Revolution of 1844"; anonymous *décimas* from the nineteenth century; and Santa Anna's autobiography, *The Eagle*.

BODY

The base text used for the erasure is a section of the 2011 Arizona Revised Statutes, AZ Rev Stat § 32-1365.02 (1996 through 1st Reg Sess 50th Legis). See https://law.justia.com/codes/arizona/2011/title32/section32-136502/.

CLIMATE

276   "The really weird thing is . . ." Quoted in Mark Trahant, "How Col-

onization of the Americas Killed 90 Percent of Their Indigenous People—and Changed the Climate," *Yes! Magazine*, February 13, 2019, https://www.yesmagazine.org/opinion/2019/02/13/how-colonization -of-the-americas-killed-90-percent-of-their-indigenous-people-and -changed-the-climate/. See also Alexander Koch, Chris Brierley, Mark M. Maslin, and Simon L. Lewis, "Earth System Impacts of the European Arrival and Great Dying in the Americas After 1492," *Quaternary Science Reviews* 207 (March 1, 2019): 13–36, https://doi.org/10.1016/j .quascirev.2018.12.004.

WORKS CONSULTED, ERASED, READ, REMIXED, SAMPLED

Alarcón, Norma. "Chicana Feminism: In the Tracks of 'the' Native Woman." *Cultural Studies* 4, no. 3 (1990): 248–56.

Amerika, Mark. *Remix the Book*. Minneapolis: University of Minnesota Press, 2011.

Anaya, Rudolfo. *Billy the Kid and Other Plays*. Norman: University of Oklahoma Press, 2011.

Andreotti, Libero, and Nadir Lahiji. *The Architecture of Phantasmagoria: Specters of the City*. London: Routledge, 2017.

Anzaldúa, Gloria. *Borderlands / La Frontera: The New Mestiza*. San Francisco: Aunt Lute Books, 2012.

Anzaldúa, Gloria. *The Gloria Anzaldúa Reader*. Edited by AnaLouise Keating. Durham, N.C.: Duke University Press, 2009.

Anzaldúa, Gloria. *Light in the Dark / Luz en lo oscuro: Rewriting Identity, Spirituality, Reality*. Edited by AnaLouise Keating. Durham, N.C.: Duke University Press, 2017.

Auchter, Jessica. *The Politics of Haunting and Memory in International Relations*. New York: Routledge, 2014.

Balsom, Erika, and Hila Peleg. *Documentary Across Disciplines*. London: MIT Press, 2016.

Barthes, Roland. *Camera Lucida: Reflections on Photography*. Translated by Richard Howard. New York: Hill and Wang, 1982.

Bassett, Molly H. *The Fate of Earthly Things: Aztec Gods and God-Bodies*. Austin: University of Texas Press, 2015.

Bataille, Georges. *The Absence of Myth: Writings on Surrealism*. Edited and translated by Michael Richardson. London: Verso, 2006.

Bataille, Georges. *The Accursed Share, Volume 1*. Translated by Robert Hurley. New York: Zone Books, 1991.

Bataille, Georges. *The Accursed Share, Volumes 2 and 3*. Translated by Robert Hurley. New York: Zone Books, 1993.

Bataille, Georges. *The Bataille Reader*. Edited by Fred Botting and Scott Wilson. Oxford: Blackwell Publishing, 1997.

Bataille, Georges. *Dossier de l'oeil pinéal*. Illustrated by Micha Brendel. N.p.: Ed. Quatre en Samisdat, 1994.

Bataille, Georges. *Encyclopaedia Acephalica: Comprising the Critical Dictionary and Related Texts*. London: Atlas Press, 1995.

Bataille, Georges. *Encyclopaedia Da Costa*. Edited by Lain White and Isabelle Waldberg. London: Atlas Press, 1995.

Bataille, Georges. "Extinct America." In "Georges Bataille: Writings on Laughter, Sacrifice, Nietzsche, Un-Knowing." Special issue, *October* 36 (1986): 3–9.

Bataille, Georges. *Visions of Excess: Selected Writings, 1927–1939.* Edited by Allan Stoekl. Minneapolis: University of Minnesota Press, 1985.

Benjamin, Walter. "Theses on the Philosophy of History." Translated by Harry Zohn. In *Illuminations*, edited by Hannah Arendt, 253–65. New York: Schocken, 1969.

Besserman, Lawrence. *Sacred and Secular in Medieval and Early Modern Cultures.* New York: Palgrave Macmillan, 2006.

Biles, Jeremy. *Ecce Monstrum: Georges Bataille and the Sacrifice of Form.* New York: Fordham University Press, 2007.

Biles, Jeremy, and Kent L. Brintnall. *Negative Ecstasies: Georges Bataille and the Study of Religion.* New York: Fordham University Press, 2015.

Bolaños, Fray Joaquín. *La portentosa vida de la Muerte.* Edited by Trinidad Barrera and Jaime J. Martínez. Biblioteca Indiana. Madrid: Iberoamericana Vervuert, 2016.

Borges, Jorge Luis. *Collected Fictions.* Translated by Andrew Hurley. New York: Penguin, 1998.

Briet, Suzanne. *Qu'est-ce que la documentation?* Paris: Éditions documentaires, industrielles et techniques, 1951.

Brown, Andrew. *A Brief History of Encyclopedias from Pliny to Wikipedia.* London: Hesperus Press, 2011.

Browne, Walden. *Sahagún and the Transition to Modernity.* Norman: University of Oklahoma Press, 2000.

Bryant, Tisa, Miranda Mellis, and Kate Schatz. *Encyclopedia Volume 1 A–E.* Providence: Encyclomedia, 2006.

Buchanan, Pat. *The Death of the West: How Dying Populations and Immigrant Invasions Imperil Our Country and Civilization.* New York: Thomas Dunn Books, 2001.

Buckland, Michael. "Documentality Beyond Documents." *The Monist* 97, no. 2 (2014): 179–86.

Buckland, Michael. "Document Theory: An Introduction." Presentation at the Summer School on Records, Archives, and Memory Studies, University of Zadar, Department of Information Sciences, Zadar, Croatia, May 6–10, 2013. Preprint, November 7, 2013.

Buckland, Michael. "What Is a 'Document'?" *Journal of the American Society of Information Science* 48, no. 9 (Sept. 1997): 804–9.

Calhoun, John C. Statement to Congress. *Congressional Record*, July 29, 1849.

Cantú, Norma. "Forjando el Destino: For Emma Tenayuca." In *Meditación Fronteriza.* Tucson: University of Arizona Press, 2019.

Caplan, Jane, and John Torpey. "Introduction." In *Documenting Individual Identity: The Development of State Practices in the Modern World*, edited by Jane Caplan and John Torpey. Princeton, N.J.: Princeton University Press, 2001.

Cave, Stephen. *Immortality: The Quest to Live Forever and How It Drives Civilization.* Delaware: Skyhorse Publishing, 2017.

Cervantes, Lorna Dee. *Sueño.* San Antonio: Wings Press, 2013.

Chak, Tings. *Undocumented: The Architecture of Migrant Detention.* Montreal: The Architecture Observer, 2014.

Conomos, John, and Brad Buckley. *Erasure: The Spectre of Cultural Memory.* Oxfordshire: Libri Publishing, 2015.

Cushing, Caleb. "Mexico." *Democratic Review*, 1846, 342–58.

d'Alembert, Jean Le Rond. *Preliminary Discourse to the Encyclopedia of Diderot.* Translated by Richard N. Schwab. Chicago: University of Chicago Press, 1995.

Dardy, Claudine. *Identités de papiers.* Paris: L'Harmattan, 1998.

Day, Ronald E. *Indexing It All: The Subject in the Age of Documentation, Information, and Data.* Cambridge: MIT Press, 2014.

De León, Jason. *The Land of Open Graves: Living and Dying on the Migrant Trail.* Oakland: University of California Press, 2015.

Delgado, Richard, and Jean Stefancic, eds. *The Latino/a Condition*. New York: New York University Press, 1998.

Derrida, Jacques. *Archive Fever: A Freudian Impression*. Chicago: University of Chicago, 2017.

Derrida, Jacques. *Paper Machine*. Translated by Rachel Bowlby. Stanford: Stanford University Press, 2005.

Derrida, Jacques. *Specters of Marx*. New York: Routledge, 2006.

Duyvis, Donker. *Normalisatie op het gebied der documentatie (Standardization in the Domain of Documentation)*. NIDER publication 214. The Hague: NIDER, 1942.

Edmonson, Munro S. *Sixteenth-Century Mexico: The Work of Sahagún*. Albuquerque: University of New Mexico Press, 1974.

Edwards, Erin E. *The Modernist Corpse: Posthumanism and the Posthumous*. Minneapolis: University of Minnesota Press, 2018.

Engels, Friedrich. "Democratic Pan-Slavism: Engels Contra Bakunin." In *Marx and Engels Collected Works*, vol. 14, 156–62. Moscow: Progress Publishers, 1980.

Ferraris, Maurizio. *Documentality: Why It Is Necessary to Leave Traces*. Translated by Richard Davies. New York: Fordham University Press, 2013.

Fintoni, Monica. *The World of the Aztecs in the Florentine Codex*. Florence: Mandragora, 2007.

Flores Magón, Ricardo. "The Repercussions of a Lynching." In *Latinx Writing Los Angeles: Nonfiction Dispatches from a Decolonial Rebellion*, edited by Ignacio López-Calvo and Víctor Valle, 71–79. Lincoln: University of Nebraska Press, 2019.

Floridi, Luciano. *The Philosophy of Information*. Oxford: Oxford University Press, 2011.

García, Mario T. *Mexican Americans*. New Haven: Yale University Press, 1989.

Garone Gravier, Marina. "The Visual Construction of a Historical Narrative: Book Design and Calligraphy of the Florentine Codex." In *Manuscript Cultures of Colonial Mexico and Peru: New Questions and Approaches*, edited by Thomas B. F. Cummins, Emily A. Engel, Barbara Anderson, and Juan M. Ossio A., 160–74. Los Angeles: The Getty Research Institute Publications Program, 2014.

Gasché, Rodolphe. *Georges Bataille: Phenomenology and Phantasmatology*. Translated by Roland Végsö. Stanford: Stanford University Press, 2012.

Gaspar de Alba, Alicia. *Desert Blood: The Juárez Murders*. Houston: Arte Público Press, 2007.

Gitelman, Lisa. *Paper Knowledge: Toward a Media History of Documents*. Durham, N.C.: Duke University Press, 2014.

Gómez-Quiñones, Juan. *Roots of Chicano Politics, 1600–1940*. Albuquerque: University of New Mexico Press, 1994.

Gonzales-Day, Ken. *Lynching in the West: 1850–1935*. Durham, N.C.: Duke University Press, 2006.

González, Deena J. "The Treaty of Guadalupe Hidalgo." In *The Treaty of Guadalupe Hidalgo, 1848: Papers on the Sesquicentennial Symposium, 1848–1998*, edited by John Porter Bloom. Las Cruces, N.M.: Doña Ana County Historical Society, 1999.

Gou, Jeff. "Why Hispanics Live Longer." *Washington Post*, October 2, 2014.

Gutiérrez, Margo, and Matt S. Meier. *Encyclopedia of the Mexican American Civil Rights Movement*. Westport: Greenwood Press, 2000.

Heidegger, Martin. *Being and Time*. Translated by Joan Stambaugh. Albany: State University of New York Press, 2010.

Heidegger, Martin. *What Is Metaphysics?* N.p.: Jovian Press, 2016. Kindle.

Herrera, Juan Felipe. *187 Reasons Mexicanos Can't Cross the Border: Undocuments 1971–2007*. San Francisco: City Lights Books, 2007.

Holland, Sharon Patricia. *Raising the Dead: Readings of Death and (Black) Subjectivity*. Durham, N.C.: Duke University Press, 2000.

Hollingsworth, Jonathan. *Left Behind: Life and Death Along the U.S. Border*. Stockport: Dewi Lewis Publishing, 2012.

Hough, Emerson. *The Story of the Outlaw: A Study of the Western Desperado*. New York: Cooper Square Press, 2001.

Johannsen, Robert W. *To the Halls of the Montezumas: The Mexican War in the American Imagination*. Oxford: Oxford University Press, 1988.

Kafka, Ben. *The Demon of Writing: Powers and Failures of Paperwork*. New York: Zone Books, 2007.

Kamps, Ivo, Karen L. Raber, and Thomas Hallock, eds. *Early Modern Ecostudies: From the Florentine Codex to Shakespeare*. New York: Palgrave Macmillan, 2008.

Kanstroom, Daniel. *Deportation Nation: Outsiders in American History*. Cambridge, Mass.: Harvard University Press, 2007.

Kanstroom, Daniel, and M. Brinton Lykes, eds. *The New Deportations Delirium: Interdisciplinary Responses*. New York: New York University Press, 2015.

Kendall, Stuart. *Georges Bataille*. London: Reaktion Books, 2007.

Kerpel, Diana Magaloni. *The Colors of the New World: Artists, Materials, and the Creation of the Florentine Codex*. Los Angeles: The Getty Research Institute, 2014.

Koepsell, David, and Barry Smith. "Beyond Paper." *The Monist* 97, no. 2 (2014): 222–35.

Lara, Jaime. *Christian Texts for Aztecs: Art and Liturgy in Colonial Mexico*. Notre Dame: University of Notre Dame Press, 2008.

León-Portilla, Miguel. *Bernardino de Sahagún: First Anthropologist*. Translated by Mauricio J. Mixco. Norman: University of Oklahoma Press, 2002.

León-Portilla, Miguel. *The Broken Spears: The Aztec Account of the Conquest of Mexico*. Boston: Beacon Press, 1962.

Levy, David. *Scrolling Forward: Making Sense of Documents in the Digital Age*. New York: Arcade Publishing, 2001.

Lighton, William R. "The Greaser." *Atlantic Monthly* 83, no. 500 (1899): 750–56.

Lomnitz, Claudio. *Death and the Idea of Mexico*. New York: Zone Books, 2008.

López, Ian Haney. *White by Law: The Legal Construction of Race*. New York: New York University Press, 1996.

Lorentzen, Lois Ann. "*Santa Muerte*: Saint of the Dispossessed, Enemy of Church and State." *Emisférica* 13, no. 1 (2016). https://hemisphericinstitute.org/en/emisferica-13-1-states-of-devotion/13-1-essays/santa-muerte-saint-of-the-dispossessed-enemy-of-church-and-state.html.

Lucretius. *The Nature of Things*. New York: Penguin, 2007.

Malavé, Idelisse, and Esti Giordani. *Latino Stats: American Hispanics by the Numbers*. New York: The New Press, 2015.

Marx, Karl. "The Intervention in Mexico." *New York Daily Tribune*, November 23, 1861.

Marx, Karl. "On the Jewish Question." In *The Marx and Engels Reader*, edited by Robert Tucker, 158–91. New York: Norton, 1994.

Matheson, Neil, and Sas Mays. *The Machine and the Ghost: Technology and Spiritualism in Nineteenth- to Twenty-First-Century Art and Culture*. Manchester: Manchester University Press, 2013.

Mbembe, Achille. "Necropolitics." Translated by Libby Meintjes. *Public Culture* 15, no. 1 (Winter 2003): 11–40.

Menchaca, Martha. *Recovering History, Constructing Race: The Indian, Black, and White Roots of Mexican Americans*. Austin: University of Texas Press, 2002.

Mendez, et al. v. Westminister [*sic*] School District of Orange County, et al. 64 F. Supp. 544 (SD Cal 1946), *aff'd* 161 F.2d 1774 (9th Cir. 1947).

Montejano, David. *Anglos and Mexicans in the Making of Texas, 1836–1986*. Austin: University of Texas Press, 1987.

Moore, John. *Undocumented Immigration and the Militarization of the United States–Mexico Border*. Brooklyn: powerHouse Books, 2018.

Nericcio, Willliam Anthony. *Seductive Hallucinations of the "Mexican" in America*. Austin: University of Texas Press, 2007.

Nicolau d'Olwer, Luis. *Fray Bernardino de Sahagún 1499–1590*. Translated by Mauricio J. Mixco. Salt Lake City: University of Utah Press, 1987.

Ochoa O'Leary, Anna. *Undocumented Immigrants in the United States: An Encyclopedia of Their Experience, Vols. 1–2*. Santa Barbara: Greenwood Press, 2014.

O'Sullivan, John. "Annexation." *Democratic Review* 17 (1845): 234–54.

O'Sullivan, John. "The Mexican Question." *North American Review* 103, no. 212 (1847): 434–35.

Otero, Miguel Antonio. *The Real Billy the Kid: With New Light on the Lincoln County War*. New York: R. R. Wilson, 1936.

Paredes, Américo. *George Washington Gómez: A Mexicotexan Novel*. Houston: Arte Público Press, 1990.

Parker, Philip M. *Undocumented: Webster's Timeline History, 219–2007*. San Diego: Icon Group International, 2010.

Peeren, Esther. *The Spectral Metaphor: Living Ghosts and the Agency of Invisibility*. New York: Palgrave Macmillan, 2014.

Peeren, Esther, and María del Pilar Blanco. *The Spectralities Reader: Ghosts and Haunting in Contemporary Cultural Theory*. New York: Bloomsbury Academic, 2013.

Peutz, Nathalie, and Nicholas D. Genova. *The Deportation Regime: Sovereignty, Space, and the Freedom of Movement*. Durham, N.C.: Duke University Press, 2010.

Plascencia, Salvador. *The People of Paper*. New York: Mariner Books, 2006.

Prieto, Guillermo. "The Glorious Revolution of 1844." In *The Mexico Reader*, edited by Gilbert M. Joseph and Timothy J. Henderson. Durham, N.C.: Duke University Press, 2003.

Rak, Julie, and Anna Poletti. *Identity Technologies: Constructing the Self Online*. Madison: University of Wisconsin Press, 2014.

Reforming American Immigration for a Strong Economy (RAISE) Act. S. 1103. 116th Congress (2019–20). https://www.congress.gov/bill/116th-congress/senate-bill/1103/text.

Ribas-Casasayas, Alberto, and Amanda L. Petersen. *Espectros: Ghostly Hauntings in Contemporary Transhispanic Narratives*. Lewisburg: Bucknell University Press, 2016.

Rice, Felicia, Guillermo Gómez-Peña, Jennifer A. González, Gustavo Vazquez, and Zachary Watkins. *Doc/Undoc: Documentado/Undocumented Ars Shamánica Performática*. San Francisco: City Lights, 2017.

Ridi, Riccardo. "Phenomena or Noumena? Objective and Subjective Aspects in Knowledge Organization." *Knowledge Organization* 43 (2016): 239–53.

Riles, Annelise. *Documents: Artifacts of Modern Knowledge*. Ann Arbor: University of Michigan Press, 2009.

Rivera, John-Michael. *The Emergence of Mexican America: Recovering Stories of Mexican Peoplehood in U.S. Culture*. New York: New York University Press, 2006.

Rivera Garza, Cristina. *The Restless Dead: Necrowriting and Disappropriation*. Nashville: Vanderbilt University Press, 2020.

Robertson, Craig. *The Passport in America: The History of a Document*. Oxford: Oxford University Press, 2010.

Román, Ediberto. *Those Damned Immigrants: America's Hysteria over Undocumented Immigration*. New York: New York University Press, 2013.

Sahagún, Bernardino de. *Florentine Codex: General History of the Things of New Spain, Vols. 1–10*. Translated by Arthur J. O. Anderson and Charles E. Dibble. Santa Fe and Salt Lake City: The School of American Research / University of Utah Press, 1981.

Sahagún, Bernardino de. *Primeros memoriales*. Norman: University of Oklahoma Press, 1993.

Sahagún, Bernardino de. *Psalmodia christiana (Christian Psalmody)*. Translated by Arthur J. O. Anderson. Salt Lake City: University of Utah Press, 1993.

Salinas, Luis Omar. *The Sadness of Days: Selected and New Poems*. Houston: Arte Público Press, 1986.

Salün, Jean-Michel. "Why the Document Is Important . . ." *The Monist* 97, no. 2 (2014): 187–99.

Santa Anna, Antonio López de. *The Eagle: The Autobiography of Santa Anna*. Edited by Anna Fears Crawford. Austin: Pemberton Press, 1967.

Segarra, Lisa Marie, and David Johnson. "Find Out If President Trump Would Let You Immigrate to America." *Time Magazine*, August 7, 2017. https://time.com/4887574/trump-raise-act-immigration/.

Seltzer, Mark. *Bodies and Machines*. New York: Routledge, 1992.

Sharpe, Christina. *In the Wake: On Blackness and Being*. Durham, N.C.: Duke University Press, 2016.

Smith, Barry. "How to Do Things with Documents." *Rivista di Estetica* 50 (2012): 179–98.

Sontag, Susan. *On Photography*. New York: Picador, 1977.

Steedman, Carolyn. *Dust: The Archive of Cultural History*. New York: Rutgers University Press, 2002.

Steiner, Emily. *Documentary Culture and the Making of Medieval English Literature*. Cambridge: Cambridge University Press, 2003.

Stephanson, Anders. *Manifest Destiny: American Expansion and the Empire of Right*. New York: Hill and Wang, 1995.

Stephens, Paul. *The Poetics of Information Overload: From Gertrude Stein to Conceptual Writing*. Minneapolis: University of Minnesota Press, 2015.

Tatum, Stephen. *Inventing Billy the Kid: Visions of the Outlaw in America, 1881–1981*. Albuquerque: University of New Mexico Press, 1982.

Taylor, Diana. *The Archive and the Repertoire: Performing Cultural Memory in the Americas*. Durham, N.C.: Duke University Press, 2003.

Taylor, Víctor E. *Christianity, Plasticity, and Spectral Heritages*. New York: Palgrave Macmillan, 2017.

Tejada, Roberto. *Still Nowhere in an Empty Vastness*. El Paso: Noemi Press, 2019.

Tenayuca, Emma, and Homer Brooks. "The Mexican Question in the Southwest." *The Communist* 18 (March 1939).

Turkle, Sherry. *Evocative Objects: Things We Think With*. Cambridge, Mass.: MIT Press, 2007.

Turner, Frederick Jackson. *The Frontier in American History*. New York: Dover, 1996.

Valdez, Luis. *Zoot Suit and Other Plays*. Houston: Arte Público Press, 1992.

Velasquez, Pedro. *Memoir of an Eventful Expedition in Central America: Resulting in the Discovery of the Idolatrous City of Iximaya* [. . .]. New York: E. F. Applegate, 1850.

Vieira, Kate. *American by Paper: How Documents Matter in Immigrant Literacy*. Minneapolis: University of Minnesota, 2016.

von Hagen, Víctor Wolfgang. *The Aztec and Maya Papermakers*. New York: J. J. Augustin, 1943.

Webb, Clive, and William D. Carrigan. *Forgotten Dead: Mob Violence Against Mexicans in the United States, 1848–1928*. Oxford: Oxford University Press, 2013.

Whitman, Walt. *Leaves of Grass: The "Death-Bed" Edition*. New York: Modern Library, 1993.

Wolf, Gerhard, and Joseph Connors. *Colors Between Two Worlds: The Florentine Codex of Bernardino de Sahagún*. Cambridge: Harvard University Center for Italian Renaissance Studies, 2011.

IMAGES

ABOUT THE AUTHOR

John-Michael Rivera is an associate professor and writer at the University of Colorado at Boulder, where he serves as director of the Writing Program and creative research fellow of W.R.I.T.E. (Writing, Rhetoric, Information, Technology, and Ecology). He has published memoir, creative nonfiction, poetry, and scholarship. He was the curator of El Laboratorio, a literary space for Latinx writers, and was co-founder of *Shadowbox Magazine*, a literary journal for creative nonfiction.